Atlantic Sur

(Revised Edition)

by
Lester C. Boyd

Illustrations by
Raymond E. Knowles

Distributed by
Stackpole Books
Box 1831
Harrisburg, PA 17105

Stone Wall Press
1241 30th Street, N.W.
Washington, D.C. 20007

Cover and text photographs by the author.

This book is dedicated to my wife, Barbara, who has read it and loves every word.

So much so that she almost, but not quite, decided to take up surf fishing herself.

First Printing, 1976
Second Printing, 1977
Second Edition, 1982

ISBN 0-913276-36-7
LC 82-80188

Contents

Preface

One of my pleasurable pastimes on winter evenings is reading the outdoor magazines and the tales of fishing in such exotic and far-off places as the Florida Keys, the Bahamas, the Gulf Coast, Baja California, Costa Rica, the Pacific Northwest and other places where the gamefish grow large, plentiful and contentious.

For years I have read with envy, for it seemed with the business of earning a living, raising a family, and dealing with the massive problems of modern living—I would be forever doomed to fishing my own home shores.

Then one day instead of envying I decided to catalogue my angling blessings. After I have finished, I find there is no reason to envy any man.

Because my home ground is the North Atlantic Coast where the game and salt water panfish swarm as large, as plentiful, and every bit as contentious as the fish in the far off places I have read about.

Did you know that somewhere within casting distance of Atlantic shores, at any given time of year there are fish that can be caught on rod and reel?

Not anywhere at any time, but always somewhere. And at times almost anywhere.

Do you know that many of these fish present angling challenges equal to, and in some cases greater than those that excite anglers who travel the globe in search of fishing thrills?

Did you know that surf fishing in Atlantic waters is as varied as any place a jet liner can take you?

Perhaps this isn't as important to you as some other considerations, but you may be interested to know these fish are as tasty as any that swim the other oceans of the world.

I'm not just blowing spume at you. All these claims can be documented.

For some forty years now I've been shipping salt water into my waders, cracking my shins on those granite ledges, slipping on spray-slicked jetties, slogging through soft beach sand, sinking in the ooze of salt marshes, leaning on bridge rails and dozing on docks. I count myself lucky to have lived the life I've lived and fished the shores I've fished.

I've been there when the brittle January air froze the salt water in my guides and bit through all the layers of winter clothes I could get on—

When the thin sun of early spring was glinting on the whitecaps, set to dancing by a fresh March breeze—

When May's lingering days were bringing the first real warmth to the shore—

When the hot, pressing air of midsummer flattened the water and curtained the horizon with heat shimmers—

When the crisp, sparking days of September charged the air with the urgency of dying summer—

When November brought the bleak, gray, wave-tossing winds of late fall:

In the wild, stinging, body-pounding surf;

In the calm inlets fringed with marsh grass;

In sparking bays;

In racing, swirling, murky tidal rivers;

From flat, sandy beaches rearranged each year by winter storms;

From grinding, ankle-wrenching cobblestone beaches;

From granite ledges that brave and turn back the battering waves;

From stinking-at-low-tide salt marshes;

From docks and jetties and bridges;

For striped bass, bluefish, pollock, cod, tomcod, white perch, winter flounder, fluke, sand dabs, sea robins, eels, mackerel, scup, squeteague, herring, shad, smelt, tautog.

This is a book that will share some of the experiences I've had and help you fish some of the places I've fished. It is a directory of where to go and how to get there and information on bait, tackle and techniques that have proven successful. It is also a love letter to surf fishing along the Atlantic coast.

L.C.B.

Section I

The Basics

This is not the last definitive WORD on surf fishing. Surf fishing, like making love or writing a book, is an inexact science. Its rules are mostly general and flexible and not at all immune to change. The ability of any technique to produce the desired result, that of a spent gamefish drumming its tail on the shingle of an ocean beach, depends as much on the whims and fancies and often imponderable moods of said gamefish as on the perfection of your expertise. Nobody but a blamed fool would guarantee the results of any technique short of using depth charges.

The above is a disclaimer—a device used by those pompous enough to write a book about an inexact science such as surf fishing, but realistic enough to realize that no matter what is written, some sand-blasted old soaker with barnacles on his toenails is going to read it, snort, and wonder profanely where the devil that information came from.

Most surf fishermen have their own hard-won ideas about such matters as tides, wind direction, lure action and color, moon phases, astrological signs, prayers and incantations, and all the other factors that might be imposed on their chances for success. They're not too keen on book-learning.

I recall getting into a conversation with an old gaffer a few years ago in a bait shop near Plum Island, Massachusetts. I asked him if he had read a recently-published and highly-regarded book on surf fishing.

"Hell, no!" he said. "I don't fish half as good now as I know how to; why should I read a book to learn more?"

Maybe you don't fish half as good as you know how. Maybe you know all you need to know about surf fishing already. But maybe there is something in the following pages that will help you stink up your gaff some dawn when nothing you've been doing seems to be right.

If you think you are making mistakes, just remember that many fish, being the capricious and unreliable creatures they are, have ended up as fillets precisely because somebody wasn't following the prescribed rules. I once watched a surf caster on Nantucket hauling in striper after striper from a school breaking just off the beach while a half dozen others, all seasoned surf fishermen, were doing no more than irritating the calcium deposits in their shoulders.

We were all using popping plugs, and every surf fisherman knows that the proper way to work a popping plug is to make it dance across the surface in the manner of a panic-stricken baitfish.

Turned out this fellow didn't know that. What he was doing was letting the plug sink and then retrieving it slowly and evenly under water. Poor fellow never did learn he was doing it wrong.

As soon as the rest of us started doing it wrong, we caught fish too.

The only valid criteria of what's right and what's wrong in surf fishing is whether it works. If it works, it's the right way. Maybe it won't be the right way tomorrow, though. The wind can change, a heavy rainfall can change the salinity of the water running out of the inlet, a school of squid can move in, or a school of bunker can move out. Any number of things can happen. Play it loose and leave your options open, with one of these options being the completely illogical or innovative or downright foolish in case the regular tricks don't work.

Surf fishermen are generally considered to be among the advanced students of the angling arts. In the normal course of events, a man often becomes a surf fisherman after starting out in fresh water. Then, as he looks for more demanding challenges, moves to salt water and ultimately to the point where the only satisfactory way of testing his mettle is to go to the exposed rim of the ocean and there confront the surf.

To do this he needs some highly-specialized tackle, rods, reels, lines, and lures developed specifically for surf fishing.

Many surf fishermen develop their own prejudices as they come up through the ranks of the less demanding disciplines. When they arrive, they find themselves faced with making new decisions without having the proper specifications; unsure of what is best or most appropriate in the bewildering array of rods and reels offered by the manufacturers. For them there are no quick answers; because in the ocean within reach of the surf caster there are a variety of fish living under a variety of conditions.

You can't find a perfect, all-around, all purpose surf fishing outfit. Oh, I've known men who claimed to have found one, but time and usage discloses flaws.

RODS

Surf rods, for instance, range from the vaulting poles used to heave five ounces of lead and a slab of bunker far out to the slough where great, sag-bellied, bucket-mouthed striped bass are edging in with the tide to the light, one-handed rods designed to whip half-ounce jigs and plugs to the school stripers and weakfish chasing bait through the suds. In between are rods designed for every special circumstance, every style, every technique, every preference.

So wide-ranging are the demands that no one rod can do all jobs effectively. The production stick used to reach the sloughs where the cow bass are feeding is hardly appropriate for the angler who wants to present a bait or lure to the fluke waiting at the drop off. The slender popping rod whose job it is to make a popper dance across the surface would fail miserably if put to the task of hauling a reluctant tautog from its hole among the rocks.

The gradations in size and purpose of surf outfits depends on where you're fishing, what you're fishing for, and the techniques you employ. These will be taken up in other sections. But whether your goal is to break the record for shore-caught stripers or fill the freezer with fluke fillets, it's important to recognize quality tackle.

This isn't as easy as you might think. Time was, and still is in some places, where fishing tackle was sold in small specialty shops run by people who knew and cared about fishing tackle and were willing to take the time to see that the customer got tackle that was both appropriate to his needs and of good quality. But times and merchandising methods change. Today most tackle is purchased at discount department stores at a price below what the small tackle dealer has to pay for it.

I don't want to knock the discount stores, which provide a wide selection of tackle at low cost. But they do not provide the service and guidance a man can get in a small specialty store. Too often the sporting goods department manager is a budding merchant prince who is putting in his time in sporting goods while waiting for an opening in ladies ready-to-wear. To ask him what kind of tip action is best for casting bucktail jigs to small stripers and weakfish isn't going to get you much more than a blank stare.

Sound advice in these discount stores is often hard to come by. Merchandising today is geared to price rather than personal service. So how does a man pick a good, serviceable rod from a rack holding hundreds? One way is to take along someone who knows what to look for.

Brand name is often an excellent guide to quality, but even here it should be remembered that the large manufacturers produce varying

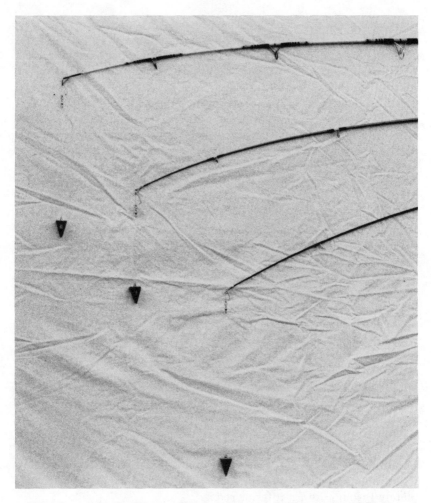

These three surf rods, all hung with four ounce weights, illustrate three different types of rod action. The rod on the top has a stiff, fast-action tip, ideal for working popping plugs. Below that is a rod with a softer, slower action tip, best for fishing swimming plugs. The bottom rod has parabolic action—the action is built into the entire length of the rod rather than just the tip. Many favor this action for bait fishing since the slow action lobs the bait rather than snapping it out. A fast action tip can snap the bait from the hook during a cast.

grades of quality, just as the automobile makers produce high and low price cars. If the manufacturer is competing in the low price field as well as the quality field, the rod you buy may not be one you'll want to live with—regardless of its good name.

Price is sometimes a dependable guide, but over-pricing is not unheard of in our profit-conscious culture.

So here are a few considerations to look for:

First the rod. Look for hollow glass rather than solid glass. (I'm discounting here split bamboo and Calcutta sticks, once popular tools but now outmoded by the synthetics, and metal rods, which never made it.) Solid glass rods have their uses, but surf fishing is not one of them. Hollow glass, while lacking the pure brawn of solid glass, is lighter, more responsive, and has better action and balance. While more fragile than solid glass, it is still plenty tough and is the best design for surf fishing.

Graphite rods are stronger, lighter, more sensitive, and have proven themselves after a decade on the beaches. Consider them if price is no object. That price, you should be warned, is at least double that of a good glass rod. Graphite rods are a delight to use. I have fly casting, bait casting and surf casting rods made of this material and constantly marvel at the ease in casting, the sensitivity of the tips. A graphite rod can add yards to your casts while requiring less effort.

My advice to a beginner would be to start with glass, learn the trade, and then invest in graphite when experience has taught you just what you want in a rod.

The hardware is perhaps the best indication of the quality of a rod.

The prime consideration here, and indeed an overriding consideration in the selection of any marine hardware, is its degree of resistance to the corrosive effects of salt water. There are a number of alloys that meet this standard. The best and most popular is aluminum oxide, a hard, corrosion-resistant material. But stainless steel guides will serve to carry soft, braided line from revolving spool reels.

Aluminum oxide is popular for spinning rods because it is hard enough to resist being cut by monofiliment line. It is particularly important in the tip eye which takes most of the wear. A softer alloy will groove quickly under hard use. I have seen tip eyes wear completely through on an inferior rod.

At one time agate was considered the best material for tip eyes and guides because it is both smooth and hard. Agate is still excellent, but it is brittle. With surf fishing being the knock-about activity it is, the life expectancy of an agate tip eye is not great. Cracked agate will quickly ruin your line.

The tip eye should be of fairly large diameter and should be solidly braced with strong legs. Look for smooth, strong welds; not soldered joints, where the braces meet the body and the eye. A large diameter serves two purposes—it permits a freer flow of line during the cast and provides more area to dissipate the heat that is generated by the swiftly-flowing line.

The guides should also be of aluminum oxide or other hard, corrosion-resistant material. Similarly, they should have strong braces and smooth, strong welds. No rod needs more than five guides, incidentally. No matter how long it is.

On a surf spinning rod the first guide, also called the gathering guide, should be about the same diameter as your reel spool. When the line flows off your reel during a cast, rather large loops are formed. If they are gathered by a small first guide, you will be creating unnecessary friction. On a standard nine or ten foot spinning rod this gathering guide should be about 26 inches from the reel seat. The remaining guides should be placed at decreasing distances toward the tip. This arrangement allows the rod to bend along its natural line of flex.

A good many rods have been sold because of attractive windings, but it should be remembered that pretty windings are not necessarily good windings. A pretty rod, like a pretty girl, can turn out to be a bad bargain.

The best rods are under-wound and then over-wound twice. You won't see many rods in discount department stores, or even in tackle stores, wound this way. Usually only custom rod makers take the trouble to underwind. Good commercial rods are generally over-wound twice, while the cheaper ones make do with but one layer of thread holding the guides. Even inexpensive rods are wound with nylon thread. It's a good idea to put an extra layer of shellac over the windings when you get your rod home, just to be on the safe side. Your rod will last longer. By the way, the windings need not extend beyond the feet of the guides, even though most rod makers dress up their products with extra windings.

The first spinning rods were made with sliding rings for reel seats, a primitive and not always satisfactory arrangement. Today most spinning rods are made with fixed reel seats that secure the reel with locking rings. The new reel seats are better in one respect; they are far less likely to let go at the very moment a bluefish is reacting to the sting of your hook. But the old sliding rings had one advantage; they allowed a fisherman to place the reel wherever it was most comfortable for him.

I have half a dozen surf rods in various sizes and only one has a fixed reel seat. This one is a medium-weight spinning rod I bought second-hand many years ago. None of the others have reel seats. I tape my reels on with plastic electrician's tape.

The placement of the reel is the only adjustment we have on a surf rod. But it is the most important one for comfort and efficiency in casting. A strong, brawny man may have the power to drive a rod forward with only short leverage. He would probably prefer to have his reel seated far down on the rod butt. A man with lesser strength would find it advantageous to move the reel farther forward to provide greater leverage. There is also the matter of arm length. A tall man with long arms would be more comfortable with the reel seat well forward.

So if you can find the rod you want with a fixed reel seat just where you want it, then that's the rod to buy. Otherwise find a rod with no reel seat and tape the reel where it is most comfortable for you. Surf fishing is a wearying enough activity without making it any more difficult. And don't worry about the tape letting go under the stress of battle. If you've wound it on properly it will hold. Some revolving spool reels come equipped with clamps that permit you to mount the reel where it is most comfortable.

If you buy a rod with a fixed reel seat make sure the metal is resistant to salt water. See to it that the slots are large enough to accomodate the reel it will be holding. There should be a locking ring in addition to the ring holding the reel.

The handle should be wound with cork. Fiberglass is slippery when wet.

I have another good reason for not having metal reel seats on my surf rods. A good deal of my surf fishing is done in the spring and fall, even into early winter. Cold metal quickly numbs my aging fingers. The tape is much easier on the fingers in cold weather.

Unless you have some compelling reason such as problems with transportation or storage, stick to one-piece rods. It's tough getting them in and out of the house or up and down the cellar stairs. Even though I've been bending them around door jambs and maneuvering them past lamps and knick-knacks for years, I prefer them over two-piece rods.

One occasional fishing buddy of mine claims to have knocked down a banjo clock in the living room an average of three times a year for the past seven years. Although he could pass his rods out through the kitchen and the back door, he insists in twisting and turning them along a tortuous path through the living room and dining room and out the front door. With good reason, he claims.

He was leaving for an overnight trip to the Charlestown Beachway in Rhode Island's South Shore one Saturday afternoon and found his customary route through the kitchen blocked because the floor was being washed and waxed. So he detoured through the front door and that night landed a 38 pound striped bass, by far the largest he had ever caught.

Being a man of quick perception he immediately saw the pattern. All the years he had been carrying his rods out the back door and had caught nothing over 12 pounds. On the one occasion he went out through the front door he caught a 38 pounder.

So for the past seven years he's been knocking down the banjo clock an average of three times a year. There's no question in his mind that it's worth the trouble. Two years later he caught a 21 pounder at the same spot and on Memorial Day of 1973 he landed a 42 pounder at the Cape Cod Canal.

You couldn't give this fellow a jointed rod.

There are two-piece, and even multiple-piece rods being built today that have fine action. The new, glass-to-glass ferrules are a big improvement over metal ferrules, and rod-making techniques are improving with every issue of spring catalogs. So don't be afraid of a break-down rod if it means saving that banjo clock rich Uncle Milton gave you. But if you have the freedom of choice, pick a one-piece weapon.

You can, if you have the wherewithall and the need, get a surf rod that will break down and fit into your suitcase. I've never used one on the beach, but I have swished them around in the tackle store and they felt fine. Some who have used them say they do the job.

There is another, and less expensive way of getting your rod. You can buy a blank, available at many specialty and department stores, and build your own. You'll save enough to buy a second rod, or the makings thereof. It's not a difficult job. I have built several, and while my expertise with winding thread is not a joy to the eye, none has ever failed me on the beach. Some of my fishing buddies with more artistry and patience produce rods that compare favorably with commercial products.

A surf rod has three basic functions—casting, retrieving and fighting a fish. A good rod must perform all three well. Casting is first in importance. You can't catch a fish your bait or lure can't reach.

The second function, retrieving, is too often not given the importance it deserves. But experienced surf fishermen know the importance of working a lure properly and how critical rod action can be in this function. I know men who carry two rods, one for working surface poppers and one for working underwater lures. Maybe you think this is carrying sophistication to the point of absurdity, but the line between surf fishing and absurdity is a thin one. Carrying one rod for working poppers and another for swimmers is not as preposterous as it might sound. We'll comment more on that later.

The third function of a rod, that of fighting a fish is, as far as I'm concerned, of less importance than the other two. Surf rods are not designed primarily to fight fish. They are designed with features that will make them efficient tools for casting and retrieving.

REELS

All right, you've got your rod, the first component of your surf fishing outfit. It's size and action have been determined by the type of fishing you will be doing. Now a reel must be fitted to the rod.

We're assuming you want a spinning reel. There are those who still prefer the old, and still useful revolving spool reels, but fewer and fewer are found as the years pass and those carrying on the old traditions leave the beach. The fact is, while we're on the subject, the revolving spool reel and the old production rod are still the best equipment for heaving four and five ounce sinkers and slabs of cut bait out to where the cow bass are feeding, or for handling such baits as eels and live bunker. But much surf fishing now is aimed at smaller targets, and spinning is a handier way of getting the job done.

Your first consideration is size. Your new reel, if it's going to balance your rod, must be neither too large nor too small. While that seems painfully obvious, I've seen some sorry rod and reel combinations on the beach.

Remember, too, that a large, fresh water reel, even a very good large, fresh water reel, is not a salt water reel. A surf reel must be built of materials that will resist the corrosive effects of salt water. Nothing less will do.

In that connection, watch out for bargains. I've bought them and been sorry. So have a lot of other people. Resign yourself to the fact that a quality surf reel, one that will do the job and stand up under the pressures, will not be cheap.

Pick up a reel and turn the handle. If you can hear the gears grinding or feel them meshing, put it down. You want a reel that is smooth and silent. Flip the bail back and then turn the handle. You'll want to hear a quick, sharp click when the bail closes — neither a slam, nor a dull, indecisive thud. The bail should spring back quickly and surely without slamming.

Unfortunately there is no sure way to test the reel drag without putting line on the reel. With any kind of luck the drag will ultimately be tested in action, and if it grabs when 30-odd pounds of streaking striper is going someplace with your plug it's too late to do anything about it. You can have some measure of assurance that a quality reel made by a reputable manufacturer will have a dependable drag.

There is one test you can run, but you must have line on the reel to do it. Just run the line over the roller bearing, set the drag lightly, and hold the line. The weight of the reel will cause it to drop slowly against the lightly set drag. If it drops smoothly, count that as a plus. If it stutters or hesitates, you don't want the reel. A roller bearing is a must for surf fishing. Make sure the roller rolls; otherwise it's useless. Keep the roller bearing lubricated with a light oil and test it by running the line over it under tension.

Most reels have their drag adjustment on the face of the spool. This is a convenient arrangement for the manufacturer, but not necessarily for the fisherman. My favorite reel has the drag setting on the heel of the casing where it can be easily seen and easily adjusted, even when fighting a fish.

It helps to have a substantial hand grip. You want more than your finger tips in the handle when you're playing a gamefish in the surf.

Get a reel with an extra spool, or, if no extra spool comes with the reel, send away for one at once. An extra spool loaded with line can be mighty handy when there's a lot of sandy miles between you and the nearest tackle store. And it is often handy to have a spool filled with heavier or lighter line to meet specific situations. Quick take-down reels make life easier on the beach. On some spinning reels the spool may be removed simply by pushing a button. On others the face must be unscrewed and the drag disassembled, inviting disaster on a dark night. Some revolving spool reels are also equipped with quick take-down devices. You'll appreciate them when you have to change a spool on the beach or jetty.

Look for adequate line capacity. Ocean-bred fish are capable of long, non-stop runs. You want to stock enough line so the fish gets tired of running it out before the bitter end goes flying through the guides.

Some reels have a built-in source of trouble you can't detect until you load it with line. The bail on any spinning reel should be engineered to lay the line on the spool evenly. Some don't. If the line builds up toward the front of the spool additional friction will be created during the cast. That's better than having it build up toward the back. When this happens you'll start throwing loops. I've got one such reel I used for two or three years. It's now a spare on the shelf. But when I was using it regularly I spent as much breath cursing it as I've spent cursing such other tribulations as editors, teen-age children, dogfish, weeds in the surf, and women drivers.

And spinning reels by nature have another built-in defect, although it is not present on all. It's the unbalanced handle which, if not positioned properly before the cast, can swing and snap the bail shut, aborting the cast abruptly. This has sent more than one $4.50 plug sailing off unattached over the blue Atlantic, and even caused some to lose rod and reel in the surf.

If you have a reel that does this consistently, remove the bail and convert it to manual pick-up.

As for revolving spool reels, it's hard to go wrong if you buy one of the several major brands. I, personally, prefer a wide-spool reel like the Penn Squidder which holds two hundred yards of 36 pound test nylon squidding line, the standard line of New England surf fishermen for many years. I've been using the same Penn Squidder now for more than 25 years and it's still holding up. Of course I don't use it nearly as much now since spinning tackle has become popular.

Few surf reels are marketed with level wind devices, and unless you are the greenest of beach pilgrims you don't want one either. Learn to lay the line on the reel with your thumb as you retrieve. After a while it will become automatic.

LINES

My surf fishing days go back to those times when the first chore after any fishing trip was to strip off the nine-thread linen line (we called it Cuttyhunk), rinse it in fresh water, and hang it in loose coils to dry. Failure to go through this pesky routine meant a short life for the line which was highly susceptible to mildew and rot.

Nobody has to do that any more. You can leave your monofiliment or nylon or Dacron braid on your reel all season if you want to and nothing much bad is going to happen as a result.

Come to think of it, when I started this book I vowed I wasn't going to recall the trials of surf fishing as it was when my generation was just starting out. I've long been tired of writers who make a point to hark back to the days of knuckle-buster reels, Calcutta rods and linen line, purely for the purpose, I suspect, of presenting themselves as grizzled veterans who have been piling up wisdom over the years. As far as I'm concerned, longevity is more of an accident than an accomplishment. It doesn't necessarily contribute to wisdom.

Oh well, I'll leave that bit about the linen line anyway. Why should this be the first book ever written about surf fishing that doesn't mention linen line?

To go on . . .

I've read some learned pieces on the molecular structure of the artificial fibers used in today's lines, their stretch properties, knot strength, limpness and other qualities, but I never really understood much of it. In the end I always did what I had always done before, go out and buy a line that looked good and wasn't too expensive.

Instead of getting bogged down in technicalities, I suggest you do the same thing. With some care in selection, of course.

Let me stress two major criteria in selecting a line—size and price. In monofiliment practically any name-brand line in the medium price range will do a decent job. I find that I chafe, wear-out, break off or otherwise ruin a high priced line just as quickly as a medium priced line, and there's not that much difference in quality. In fact I have a couple of spools filled with the cheapest line available. This suits me for bottom fishing when little or no casting is necessary. What's the point in paying $10 a hundred yards for line that's just going to be dropped into a hole in the rocks to haul out tautog?

The other criteria, size, is perhaps the most important. If the line is too heavy for your reel, it will not lay well on the spool and your casting distance will be greatly reduced. Too fine a diameter and it won't do the job.

Twenty pound test is about the heaviest you should go in spinning. Above that and the diameter of the line is such that it becomes difficult to handle. Most of my surf spools are filled with 12 or 15 pound test. I carry 20 pound line on just one surf reel, an old coffee grinder mounted on an 11½ foot meat rod I use for bait fishing when I need to make distance.

If you're worried about a fish snapping your 12 or 15 pound test line, just look at the International Game Fish Association records for fish such as bass, blues, weaks and tautog on those line classifications. Of course many of those records were set from boats where the angler had the advantage of a moveable platform. But any surf fisherman with a reliable drag on his reel, a full spool, some basic expertise and luck with him can whip just about anything he's likely to tie onto in the surf on a 12 or 15 pound test line. It just takes a little longer.

For my revolving spool reels I prefer 36 pound test flat-braided nylon squidding line, mostly because that's what I've been using for years and I'm accustomed to it. Some prefer Dacron and some put monofiliment on their revolving spool reels.

Some Cape Codders prefer 45 pound test squidding line. Insurance, perhaps, against losing that world record striper that is sure to be hooked in Cape water one of these days. The 45 pound line enables a fisherman to horse in an average fish without wasting time, important when there is a school of bass or blues working under bait within casting range. I really can't see any other advantage to it.

In choosing a line, look for some degree of limpness. The knot strength is decreased in a limp line, and its tendency to stretch will be more pronounced. However, it will give you longer casts, often important in surf fishing where your approach to the spot where gamefish are feeding is limited by your willingness to ship water in your waders. And it will give you more trouble-free casting.

You can overcome the knot strength deficiency by using a Bimini hitch. A few years ago I tested every knot I knew on a testing machine and found that a Bimini hitch and a cinch knot were the only combination that would consistently hold until the line broke. No matter how many times I tried it on lines of various weights, if the knots were properly tied they refused to slip or break.

The trouble with a Bimini hitch is that it's much easier to tie at home than on the end of a jetty on a dark night in a 15 knot wind. Here's how I do it. Seated in a chair I lean the rod over my left shoulder and run the line across the back of my neck, over my right shoulder, down the left side of my right leg, under my foot and then up the outside of my right leg.

Then the phone rings.

To tie the knot, hold the standing part of the line in your left hand and the end in your right. Wrap the end ten times up the standing end and ten times down; tie a half hitch around each leg, then another half hitch around both legs and you have it. Make sure when you tie on whatever terminal tackle you're using that the legs are even when you tie your cinch knot. Otherwise only one strand will be working. This knot gives you the added advantage of a double line for the last couple of feet, eliminating the need for a shock leader.

New manufacturing processes have eliminated much of the stretch that was built into monofiliment lines when they first hit the market, but some remains. This can give you grief, especially if your reel has a plastic spool. Fighting a big fish puts great stress on a mono line, which will stretch and shrink in diameter. When it's back on the spool it will tend to return to its original diameter. The spool can literally explode! It's not a pretty sight.

To avoid this, don't leave your line on the spool after unusual stress. A few casts will bring it back to its original diameter. Of course if you hook another big fish on the next cast you'll have the same

The ultimate end of a fish line. There are more than 20 different lines in this tangle found on a Jersey beach.

problem all over again, but I've never heard anyone complain when that happened.

Also be careful of twists in the line. This is a frequent problem for trollers who don't use a keel and good swivels when trolling spinning baits and lures. It also happens to surf casters at times. The twist occurs when your drag is loose and you keep reeling a fish without gaining line. Every turn of the bail is putting another twist in your line. It once happened to one of my lines. I let another fellow borrow one of my outfits. He loosened the drag and then hooked a good bluefish in the surf at Montauk. I watched him reel and reel without getting the fish in before we realized the fish wasn't coming in at all. I had him tighten the drag. After he landed the fish I had to retire the line.

Like many other surf fishermen I buy my line in bulk. It's cheaper that way and if your line gets nicked on the rocks or shortened too many times because it was hung up and broken off, it's easy to fill your reel spool again. Fill your spools by taking the line off the original spool over the end, making sure it is coming off in the same direction it's going on your reel. This avoids twisting.

Line is cheap. You can fill a reel spool with good line for a buck or so if you buy it in bulk; so don't hesitate to throw away your old line and put on new if your reel spool gets low or if your line gets nicked. A properly filled spool means trouble-free casting.

If it is too full, you'll be throwing loops. If not full enough your casts will be shortened. So fill it until the line comes to within an eighth of an inch of the lip.

The only time I ever saw a man throw his rod in the water was the result of an improperly filled spool. I was walking Plum Island Beach in Massachusetts and stopped to chat with a fellow who was baiting with a sea worm. His reel, I noticed, was only about half full. I considered suggesting to him that he might have trouble casting, but decided to mind my own business. He walked down to the water, wound up, made a prodigious cast, and the line somehow jammed coming off the reel. His terminal tackle broke off and flew out to sea, followed almost immediately by the rod and reel.

While the synthetic lines are just about impervious to rot, they are weakened if exposed to the sun for any length of time. They become brittle and break easily; so store them where the sun won't hit them. Cold weather also tends to stiffen monofiliment lines, making them a little more difficult to cast.

MISCELLANEOUS GEAR

There are a few more pieces of equipment you should have before you go fishing. One is a bag of some sort to carry your lures and/or bottom rigs. About the best I've found are those bags with compartmented inserts. If you're using artificial lures it's handy to have the lures on you so you can roam the beach at will. Since many artificials have treble hooks that are prone to tangle with other hooks, the compartmented bags keep the hooks apart. If you're bait fishing, a tackle box will serve to hold your gear. Make sure it's a plastic box. I never saw a metal box that was worth a damn on the beach.

For jetty fishing you should have a long-handled gaff. Paint the handle white or use phosphorescent paint if you're going to do much night fishing. A gaff isn't necessary for beach fishing since you can beach your fish easily enough, but many carry them nevertheless. After trying quite a few gimmicks, I finally devised one that would keep the hook from puncturing my waders and still have the gaff ready for use without fumbling with a cork. Take a section of surgical tubing, wind one end to the shaft with heavy twine, and slip the other end over the point of the hook. The tubing slips off the end of the hook easily when you want to gaff a fish. Yet it's right there to cover the point again.

I like to hang the gaff on my belt. Attached to the gaff and to my belt is a long elastic cord. I can grab the gaff and use it freely while it is always attached to my belt. Clever, huh?

For night fishing get one of those miner's lamps and hang it around your neck. It leaves your hands free and the light is always shining where you want it.

A knife and/or a pair of pliers on your belt are handy tools. Both should be stainless steel. A military style web belt is perfect for the job. You can hang lots of other handy tools there also.

That's your basic equipment. Now we'll look at what goes on the end of your line.

A compartmented beach bag with a typical selection of plugs and jigs used in New England. Note reel is taped to the rod.

Section 2

Lures

What you tie onto the end of your line is the most important component of your outfit. If you're not casting something that appeals to the fish, the quality of your tackle or the excellence of your expertise will mean nothing.

The ocean is a bountiful environment. So our choices of offerings to gamefish are wide, even bewildering, unless we have some idea of where to start. The body of literature of marine fishing grows annually, our knowledge of the ocean and its creatures increases, and our fishing technology becomes more refined. But the ocean still retains many secrets.

We can translate some of this knowledge to help us decide what artificial lures to use and when and how to use them. Let's look at plugs first.

At this moment, hanging on wires stretched across my corner of the cellar are upwards of 100 salt water plugs. Another 50 or so are packed in assorted jig bags and tackle boxes. In addition, a small closet holds a couple of dozen more than are still in their original packages. If there's one thing I've got, it's plugs.

Someone once suggested that I inventory all my fishing tackle for insurance purposes, which is not a bad idea, particularly since I've occasionally noted arson in my wife's eye as she passes my corner of the cellar on her way to the washing machine. Slothfulness and procrastination, however, will probably never allow it to be done.

The point is that it's easy to wind up with more fishing hardware than you'll ever use. Or have use for. No one is an easier mark for a new gadget than a fisherman — a man who will curse the kids for contributing to his financial ruin by leaving the porch light on all night while he goes out and pays $5.75 for a Super Sonic Death Darter Striper Wiper Outer because he heard someone caught a 28 pounder on one down at the inlet last week. You think that's not so? A few years ago somebody came out with a plug in the shape of a mermaid, a creature a striper or blue rarely sees and which is not a regular part of their diet. People bought them. I don't know as anyone ever caught a fish on one. I know I didn't.

Just about every baitfish that swims has been duplicated in wood or plastic. Some plugs look like no particular baitfish at all. They catch fish. Some represent certain species. They catch fish, too. Some plugs are made to wobble, some wriggle, some flash from side to side along the longitudinal axis. Some don't do much of anything unless the fisherman imparts action with his rod tip, some plugs dig deep, some just laze along the surface, some sink when at rest, some float. There are plugs with large lips, plugs with small lips, plugs with no lips at all. Some plugs have dished-in faces designed to kick up a rumpus when retrieved across the surface, others have flat or rounded noses. They come in every conceivable color and every year there are new designs to add to this bewildering array.

Given the right circumstances any one of them will catch fish. Some are better than others. Some take fish one year, but fail the next.

And in spite of the care and engineering that go into good plugs, a surf fisherman will often buy one, bend the wobble plate down, the pull eye up, paint it a different color, re-position the hooks and add a bucktail before getting it wet.

A couple of decades ago Atom Manufacturing came out with an amber colored swimming plug. It was a good lure which caught fish. But some tinkering surf fisherman came up with the crazy idea that it would catch more fish if it were towed backward. Sure enough, he was right. After a season or so the manufacturer began to rig them backward and for a while the Reverse Atom was one of the most popular and productive lures on the Southern New England Coast. It still works, given the right circumstances when the bass and blues are feeding on squid.

In fishing the Atlantic surf from Assateague Island in Maryland to Popham Beach in Maine, one is struck with regional preferences. One of the most notable being the Southern New England preference for plugs over any other lure or bait.

Walk into a tackle shop in, say Orleans, Mass. or Narragansett, R.I. and you'll see display cases and peg boards loaded with a variety of salt water plugs. Walk into a bait shop at Cape May, N.J. or Dewey Beach, Delaware, and bottom rigs will predominate. Plugs are available, but they are fewer in number and variety.

There are a couple of reasons for Southern New England's preference for plugs. The area was the birthplace of modern salt water plugging. Two pioneers in the field, Stan Gibbs and Bob Pond, had their beginnings after a few innovative striper fishermen found that large fresh water plugs such as the Creek Cub Pikie Minnow

Here are some of the oldies, plugs 25 years old or more, and the reel used to cast them.

would take fish in the Cape Cod Canal. Both Gibbs and Pond began by turning out a few plugs for themselves, then began furnishing them to friends, and eventually went into the business full time. Their plugs are still among the best.

Another reason: Along the southern New England Coast surf fishing means, almost exclusively, stripers and blues; gamesters whose dietary preferences make them pushovers for well-engineered, properly worked plugs.

The first plugs, which arrived on the scene shortly after the end of World War II (the idea of plugs wasn't brand new, for surf fishermen had been casting blocks of cedar fitted with hooks for some time) were sizeable affairs designed to be thrown with the heavy surf tackle then in use. Later, as spinning tackle became popular, smaller plugs evolved. Today plugs range from the tiny (for salt water) 5/8 ounce creations designed to interest school stripers and weakfish all the way up to plastic versions of the earlier models.

Salt water plugs fall into two basic catagories, each of which has several sub categories. There are the surface plugs which include the poppers, the splashers, and the sliders. The second category of underwater plugs include several versions of surface and underwater swimmers and darting plugs.

The surface poppers have dished-in faces that kick up a bow wave when the lure is retrieved. Most wear bucktails and most sink when at rest. The splashers have flaptails which kick up a commotion, or propellers on the nose to stir up the water. These plugs are attention-getters that are favored for daytime use. The sliders are streamlined and don't do much of anything unless worked by the rod tip.

Surface swimmers, as the name implies, go through their teasing act on, or just under the surface. They don't splash, gurgle, or kick up spray. They just swim along. The sub-surface swimmers go deeper; just how deep depends on their design. Darting plugs, akin to the surface family of plugs in that they wear no lips or wobble plates, have shelved heads that give them an erratic, darting motion.

Many plugs have had their days of glory only to fade and become just another weapon to be stored in the tackle bag and brought out only on those occasions when current favorites are not working. An exception seems to be the Finnish minnow plugs, pioneered by Rapala, brought to popularity by Rebel, and now copied by other manufacturers. Their popularity continues after more than a decade; probably because they continue to catch fish. Along the New Jersey shore today pluggers will tell you that a plug called the Redfin, a member of that same family, is the best plug you can use. I hadn't seen it in New England tackle stores, so a few years ago I brought a few back to try in Rhode Island and Massachusetts waters. They worked.

Other standard lures found in the surf bags of New England anglers include some that have been around for many years. Atom's Striper Swiper, for instance, is probably the most widely-used surface popper with the Gibbs Popper a close second.

Some surf regulars make their own plugs. Tom Morrison of Foxboro, Mass., for instance, turns out surface poppers that will outfish any commercial lure I've ever tried. He is only one of many who turn long winter evenings to profit in this manner.

A good plug consistently catches fish and will also stand up well under the wear and tear of surf fishing. Why does one plug catch more fish than another? Obvious. Because it looks and acts more like something a gamefish wants to eat. But there's another reason. One plug may be catching more fish than another because the man using the first plug knows how to use it.

Some years ago when the Finnish minnow plugs first appeared a local manufacturer confided to me that they were taking hearty chunks out of his market. "But they're idiot plugs," he said. "All you've got to do is throw them out and reel them in and they catch fish. If someone will take the trouble to learn how to work my plugs, he'll take more fish every time."

John Thorp, a neighbor, wanted to catch a striped bass. Moreover he wanted to catch it in the surf on an artificial lure. So I agreed to take him to a place where he might catch a striper in the surf, reveal unto him some of the mysteries of surf fishing, and in general give him the benefit of my expertise. But I warned him that surf fishing is a demanding discipline and cautioned him against expecting instant success.

There was a fair sea breeze whipping into the rocky Narragansett shoreline that day, but this would pose no special problem since I intended to use surface poppers (scrounged from my friend, the manufacturer, by the way). These were solidly-constructed plugs that would cast well into a headwind.

"Will they hit these?" my protege asked. He had some of those Finnish minnow plugs.

"I don't see why not," I told him, "But they're too light to cast into this wind. Better take one of my poppers."

John said no. That rock-studded water looked like a sure trap for plugs. If he was going to lose any he preferred to use his own.

His first cast should have demonstrated to him the folly of this decision. He sent the plug sailing out over the water. The wind caught it, set it fluttering like a falling leaf, and the plug splashed down a mere 40 feet away. I shrugged, decided to leave him to deal with the problem as he saw fit, and moved down the shoreline a few yards. My popping plug was drilled into the wind and consistently landing in what I felt would be productive water.

John soon shouted, "Hey, I got one!" He had a school bass that barely made the 16 inch minimum limit, but a striper nevertheless. I put it down as one of the odd events that are always happening in surf fishing and went back to work with my popping plug.

Then he caught another, a little bigger this time. Both fish had come from the wash almost at his feet. I moved closer and shortened my casts. Now my plug was working the same water as his. When he caught his third fish I put the popper away and borrowed one of his plugs. But the fish were gone. Neither of us caught another.

He was gracious about the whole affair. On the way home he thanked me for my tutelage. I was driving in traffic at the time and couldn't look at him. But I suspect he was smiling.

So some fish are caught by dumb luck and idiot plugs. I still think knowledge and experience will beat either in the long run. But why, if mankind is so smart, don't we catch more fish? How come the most common ailment among surf fishermen, ranking even above salt water rot, calcified shoulder joints and divorce, is acute frustration?

I suspect it is because no one yet has been able to detect and analyze all the factors that guide and direct fish behavior. If somebody ever does, we'll know why the fish will hit one plug on the morning tide, another on the evening tide, and nothing at all the next day. This will also take a lot of the fun out of fishing.

From what we do know we can set up a few general rules for plug casters—mighty few and mighty general. I know of only one inflexible rule for surf fishermen, **Don't wade out too far**. If I had a dime for every time that rule is broken in the course of a season I could throw away this broken down typewriter and go fishing the rest of my life.

NIGHT FISHING

The rule that seems to hold true anywhere along the coast, especially when striped bass is the prey is this: Surface disturbing plugs such as poppers and splashers should be fished only in the daytime. At night use only swimming plugs and retrieve them as slowly as you know how. How slow? A good rule is to slow the retrieve to the point where the plug is barely making headway.

I know one successful fisherman who will retrieve by letting the weight of his line move the plug forward. Then he will turn the reel handle only enough to tighten the line and stop to let the weight of the sagging line move the plug forward again. This method, of course, can be used only in a flat calm and is more useful in the quiet bays and rivers than in the surf. This is merely an illustration of just how slow slow can be.

At any rate I have proven to my own satisfaction that the rule, surface plugs by day and swimmers slowly by night, is a valid one.

Here is my special theory, which is supported by many nights spent casting plugs, rigged eels, and other tempters into the surf:

If you have fished the ocean at night you will know about phosphorescence. Scientists call it bio-luminescence and fishermen call it "fire". Striper fishermen are apt to add a few testy modifiers that are well enough known so they need not be repeated here.

According to the Encyclopedia Britannica, "fire" is caused by microscopic one-celled creatures in the zooplankton. The guilty party goes by the somewhat musical name of *Noctiluca.* This tiny sea-going firefly hates to be disturbed. Left undisturbed, he'll drift along peacefully with lights out. But disturb the water and he shoots sparks.

An outboard motor running through the nighttime water will leave a trail like a silvery comet. A plug that agitates the water puts on a fiery display that would be visible to a striper a dozen waves away. There are bass pluggers who simply shoulder their rods and walk away when the surf is filled with fire. No need for you to do that. For one thing, you can try bait fishing, or you can adapt your plugging techniques to suit the conditions.

Fish use sight, smell, and a form of hearing to find their prey. The "hearing" is the ability of a fish to pick up vibrations in the water much as our ears pick up sound waves in the air. The lateral line of the fish is the sensing organ. Tests have shown that fish can pick up the vibrations caused by the movements of another fish. They can not only determine where the stranger is, but its size as well.

Now, fish are wild creatures whose success at survival depends on their being keenly aware of all that happens in their environment. Instinct tells them when something in the environment is not as it should be. A deer feeding in a forest clearing will hear, but ignore, all the usual forest sounds. Let the sound of a striking match or a rifle hammer click reach his ears, and the tail goes up and the animal flees.

A bait fish cruising the shallows at night moves slowly by instinct. A sudden move on his part would betray his presence, both by striking sparks in the luminescent plankton and sending out easily-read vibrations. He knows it's pure suicide to advertise his presence in a world populated by bigger fish that would just love to eat him.

A predator has reasons for being unobtrusive. He lives by preying on smaller fish. There is no point in thrashing about, lighting lights, and sending out vibrations that will alert any prey. So predator fish as well would tend to move about on the aquatic equivalent of tiptoes.

The undersea world at night is a place of cautious, deliberate movement with both predator and prey keenly aware that the other is somewhere about.

When this quiet world is broken by a surface lure streaking across the surface, or a vibrating swimming plug shooting off sparks like a Roman candle, shock waves bounce off the sensors of resident fish like thunderclaps hitting an eardrum. My theory simply is that any predator will bolt—not because he recognizes the commotion as an artificial lure, but because the fish recognizes something unnatural. Anything that doesn't fit into his natural environment is bound to give him the willies.

But a swimming plug sliding quietly along, sending out vibrations like a cautious baitfish without disturbing the luminescent plankton is perfectly natural. Nothing here would frighten off a predator any more than a rabbit hopping into the clearing would frighten off a deer.

Bluefish and weaks, less circumspect than stripers, are not quite so fussy about a slow nighttime retrieve. I have often caught both at night while fishing for stripers, however; so they do respond to similar tactics. And on at least one occasion I found bluefish that ignored any plug but one that was barely moving through the dark water.

One September night on Rhode Island's Charlestown Beach was without moon or stars. So dark, in fact, that fishermen close on either side of me were out of sight. The only light anywhere was the quicksilver that glowed when one of the low swells rumbled softly against the beach.

I wasn't after bluefish that night, I was after stripers. Consequently I worked my swimming plug in the manner prescribed for dark nights when the sea is still and the water is full of fire. I caught seven bluefish on seven consecutive casts. Then, by way of experimenting, I quickened my retrieve. I moved the same swimming plug more in the order of a baitfish which, finding itself in uncomfortable proximity to a school of blues, would be concerned with getting out of there as quickly as possible. A half dozen casts produced nothing. So I went back to my slow retrieve and caught two more before the school moved on.

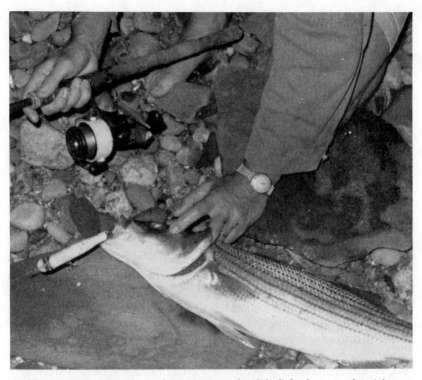

This Narragansett striper took a swimming plug fished slowly on a calm night.

Fishing at the mouth of the North River in Cape Cod Bay one night, Tom Morrison found that the normal, quick response to a strike was getting him nowhere. Tom is a pro at nighttime bassing. The best I know. When others are racking their rods in disgust because of fire in the water, Tom will persist. If the fish are there, he'll catch them.

The occasional, distinctive slap of feeding bass told him the fish were there and feeding in the dark water. The bumps he felt told him they had at least some interest in his slowly-moving swimmer. Nevertheless he was not scoring.

Finally, in desperation he tried letting his plug lie dead on the water after he felt a bump. Precisely four seconds later there would be another tug. On this second nudge he could strike and sink hooks into flesh. He ultimately discovered he could stop his plug after a bump, count to four, and then strike without waiting for the second hit.

The fish were apparently slapping the bait with their tails to stun it before turning and taking it. The turning and grabbing process took just four seconds. If the bass turned and found the baitfish, in this case Tom's plug, moving rapidly away, they presumably moved on to one that would stay knocked out long enough to be eaten.

All right, now you're convinced that when nights are dark and the sea is calm you're going to use a surface swimmer and you're going to work it as slowly as you know how. If this technique doesn't work for you, don't try getting your money back on this book. By the time you get around to giving it a fair trial I'll have spent the royalties from your copy on that 36 foot twin-screw sport fisherman I've got my eye on.

The trouble is, this crawling retrieve fits only one set of circumstances—dark nights when the sea is still and dark. Unfortunately, still nights are not that easy to come by in the surf. The normal state of the surf is troubled at best, turmoil most of the time, and serenity only occasionally. Even when there is no wind, an offshore storm can send waves crashing the bars and churning the water in the slough.

The summertime Bermuda High can settle in and deliver day after day of brisk, onshore winds. A fall line storm can whip the surf into a lather for days. Local squalls can kick up a breeze that will pluck your fishing hat right off your head and brew a chop that will make the dark sea dance with living fire. A full moon can make hammered silver of the wave tops and erase the phosphoresence as the rising sun wipes out the stars. Furthermore, the ever-present tide, racing along the beach, can be tripped up by a submerged boulder, a reef, a sandbar, even a sunken dory. Rips form, and there goes your still undersea world.

What do you do on these nights? Do what I do. Try something different.

Like the night a jillion candlepower moon lit the North Jersey landscape like it was a night game at Shea Stadium. Disregarding the surfman's dogma that block tin squid are daytime lures only, I stood on the north jetty at the Shark River Inlet and caught striped bass until my arms ached.

On a sullen August night when lightning outlined the Point Judith lighthouse and squalls tossed rain and spray into my face, a bullet-headed surface slider retrieved at flank speed took bass and blues.

Where a tide rip churned the water over a bar on Cape Cod's Nauset Beach I spent the top half of the incoming tide whipping a darting plug through the turbulence. Time after time it was nailed by stripers.

At Long Island's Shinnecock Inlet where the dark water raced out to clash with the incoming waves, on a night as black as an editor's heart, a rapidly worked bucktail jig dressed with a piece of fluttering pork rind attracted members of a mixed school of stripers and weakfish that sported in the boiling water.

Whenever the night is neither still nor dark, your options are increased. You can use lures that move rapidly, because now a swiftly-moving baitfish would not be alien. I suspect a butterfish, for instance, finding itself swept into a rip populated by stripers and blues, would immediately execute that traditional naval maneuver known as getting the hell out of there. Never mind the sparks and vibrations!

There is a practical aspect to using more active lures in moving water. When waves are charging up the beach it is virtually impossible to fish a plug slowly. It would be so tossed by the waves it would lose any resemblance to a swimming baitfish. When the high surf is running, your plug must move fast enough to bite into the water. It should keep pace with the incoming waves. Almost any swimming plug is appropriate where the water is active because of wave or tidal action.

But not surface poppers. It is an article of faith in my home waters that you don't use poppers at night. Whether it's right or wrong, I can't break with that tradition. As my grandmother would say—I was brought up better than that. If you insist in using a surface popper at night, go ahead. But if you catch any fish on it, I don't want to hear about it.

Another point while we're on the subject of night fishing. About the handiest way there is to get yourself cursed on a beach at night is to shine your light out over the water. Surf men are convinced that a light flashed on the water will spook feeding fish. I won't attest to the validity of this conviction. I've never seen it proven one way or another. But most surf men regard it as gospel and tend to get edgy, if not downright abusive, when some unthinking fisherman allows the beam of his light to hit the water while he's changing lures or untangling a snarl.

Most agree, on the other hand, that a constant light doesn't bother these fish at all. A steady light will draw baitfish. And if there's anything that will attract predators to a given vicinity it is a concentration of baitfish. Fishermen regularly take fish under the lights that line the Cape Cod Canal. Moreover, regularly flashing lights in lighthouses don't bother the fish, and there are boardwalks with street lights all along the Jersey coast which don't interfere with the night fishing.

Bill Ahern, the Westport, Mass., quahog treader, crab snatcher and striper fisherman, often turns this to his advantage. His summer home is close to the Westport Yacht Club. As a member and former commodore of the club it is his privilege to use the docks at his pleasure. So what he does when he wants a bass or two for tomorrow's dinner is walk down to the dock at night, turn on the floodlight at the end of the dock, go back to the cottage for a while to let the fish gather, and then go back and catch one or two.

There was the night that Bill was alone in the cottage. Alone, that is, except for a friendly bottle of scotch. He decided to relieve the boredom by catching a bass or two. So he strolled to the dock, lit the floodlight, and went back to the cottage and the company of the bottle to give the fish a chance to gather. When he judged an appropriate time had passed, he picked up his rod and went back to the dock where clouds of bait were darting through the lightened water. Below there were dark shadows Bill knew would be predators. He made a cast with a deep-running swimmer, drew a strike, and was fast to what he supposed would be tomorrow's dinner.

But this striper — it was a fish of perhaps ten or a dozen pounds, Bill said — was an obstreperous son-of-a-gun and an unorthodox battler as well. Instead of heading out into the river as any sensible bass would do, he decided safety lay under the dock. He bolted in that direction and before long he was tethered like a puppy with its leash wrapped around a bush. The line was wrapped around the pilings.

Bill pondered the situation a bit and concluded that the only way he was going to get that fish, along with his plug, was to go in after it. So he laid his rod and reel on the dock, hurried back to his own landing, got in his skiff, and rowed back. He took his rod from the dock and by much maneuvering and passing the rod around pilings he managed to get the fish out into the open water where he could deal with it.

The fish was now pretty well played out. Bill lifted it with the gaff. It was not securely gaffed and fell off, the hooks pulled out and the fish swam off to heal and to lead a new life that would be lived far from docks and pilings and floodlights. This left poor Bill with nothing to do but row back home and consult again with the bottle of scotch.

But Bill, being a fisherman and Irish to boot, could not stay long depressed or defeated. After a while the old spirit returned. One does not deal with adversity by brooding over it; one takes that which fate deals, absorbs the injuries, the indignities, the kicks in the spiritual kneecap, and goes back for more.

Which is just what Bill did. He picked up his rod and walked, not quite so steadily this time, back to the yacht club dock, leaned over to see if any fish were about and did just what any fisherman loaded to the eyes with scotch would do. He fell in.

Which proves, to my satisfaction, at least, that while stripers may or may not spook at a flashing light, they will tolerate a steady light that gathers bait for them to feast upon. I suppose there is also a lesson here having to do with mixing scotch and fishing. But not being a moralist, I'll leave that for the reader to deal with. Anyway, I prefer bourbon.

DAYTIME PLUG FISHING

Daytime plugging opens more options to the surf fisherman. Whether it produces more fish is open to question. That depends on the season, the area, and what you're fishing for. Probably the most popular daytime plug is the surface popper, a plug with a dished-in face designed to chug across the water creating a commotion that will hopefully come to the attention of a gamefish lurking below.

The size and depth of a popping plug's face, the part that plows into the water, determines its action. Plugs with deep, wide faces, such as the Point Jude Pop Dinger and the Arbogast Scudder, (seen on the next page), wallow through the water like a fat man doing the dog paddle. Great amounts of water are thrown around and commotion is created with very little rod work.

In fact the designer of the Pop Dinger came up with his deep dish face specifically for lady fishermen who, he says, have less trouble creating a bow wave effect with it.

Other plugs have beveled faces. The homemade plug shown on the following page is designed with a bevel from the top and a sharp lip at the bottom. This plug, made by Tom Morrison, does not stir up as much commotion as some, but when worked properly has a tantalizing action that seems to excite the fish. A carefully-weighed slug of lead in the rear gives this plug just enough weight to sink slowly when at rest.

The Striper Swiper, a standard in New England surf bags for more than a generation, has undergone a change. Pictured here is a standard model. The newer ones are designed with a much deeper face that creates a gurgling noise. Called the Talking Atom, it may or may not be more effective than the long-proven standard model.

Generally the more radical the scoop the less rod work is needed to stir things up. Pencil popper type plugs—long, slim top water runners—agitate the water very little unless some effort is put into the retrieve. The bullet-headed surface sliders, not found in many surf bags, slip through the water quietly.

The traditional way to fish a popper is to use the rod tip to make the plug fairly dance across the water, throwing up a bow wave, darting and jumping. This is supposed to represent an injured or panic-stricken baitfish streaking across the surface. It frequently convinces a striper, blue, or weakfish that this is precisely what it is. Although in almost 30 years of surf fishing I've never seen a baitfish throw up a bow wave, panic stricken or otherwise.

Since baitfish trying to escape often break water, the predator is undoubtedly attracted to the scene by this splashing. Thus, while baitfish don't throw up a bow wave, the splashing and surface agitation certainly is not out of place in the aquatic environment.

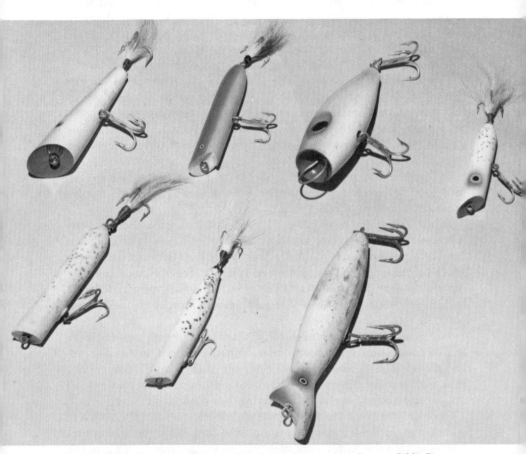

Popping Plugs: Bottom row, left to right—Striper Swiper, Atop Popper, Gibbs Popper.

Top Row, left to right—Point Jude Pop Dinger, Homemade popper, Arbogast Scudder, Point Jude Pop Along.

A popping plug is best worked with a rod that has quick tip action. Generally, you'll want your popper to dart quickly and decisively. A soft action rod tip doesn't do the job adequately. This is why some surf fishermen carry two rods, one with quick tip action for fishing poppers and one with a soft action for fishing swimming plugs.

Try it yourself and you'll see why. There is a lag between the time you whip your rod tip and the response of the plug if your rod has a soft tip action. This takes some of the life from your popper. With a swimming plug, which normally calls for a steady retrieve, this quick response isn't important. In fact it could impart a jerky action you don't want.

Don't get locked in to any single method of fishing a surface popper. There is no standard retrieve that will tempt all fish under all conditions. Normally with a popper I start my retrieve just before the plug hits the water. This takes up any slack line and sets the plug in motion immediately. A popping plug splashing down and then doing nothing except sinking slowly isn't going to convince a predator fish that it's worth investigating. Don't forget about the Nantucket fisherman who used his popper as an underwater swimmer. You never know until you experiment.

Fishing Plum Island in Massachusetts one fall morning several years ago we found the stripers were interested in our popping plugs only if they were retrieved steadily and slowly. Several weeks later, plugging from the north jetty of Barnegat Inlet, no fish would hit unless the plug acted like a spring loaded jack-in-the-box.

I offer no explanation for why the Plum Island stripers wanted their plugs served up one way while the New Jersey stripers wanted something else. This could even have been the same school of stripers since the fall migration was underway. Whatever the reason, we can draw a very important lesson here. Vary your retrieve. Try everything from yanking the plug clear out of the water to a slow and steady retrieve. Something might work.

In using flaptail plugs or plugs with head or tail propellers (neither of which seems to have won wide popularity with surf casters), a steady retrieve is in order. These plugs have built-in agitation that is sometimes attractive to gamefish. Back in the 1950's the late Joe Tartorie of Narragansett produced a flaptail plug that was highly successful. It's been a long time out of production. I lost my last one a couple of years ago to something, I suspect it was a big bluefish, at Shinnecock Inlet on Long Island.

There's not much that can be said about using these plugs. They require little in the way of rod action to make them work. Sometimes varying the speed can make the difference. In this respect, don't be afraid you're retrieving too fast for a gamefish to catch your lure. The reel hasn't been invented that can winch a plug away from a gamefish that really wants it.

Color in surface plugs doesn't seem to be as critical as it is in underwater plugs. All the gamefish sees as the plug streaks across the surface is the underside which is invariably colored white. Perhaps a contrasting color might do a better job.

Many years ago when my favorite pastime was fresh water black bass fishing, I wondered why a black surface plug was more effective on a dark night. So one night I stripped, swam out, and had a friend cast plugs of different colors over me while I watched from under water. The black plug was much more visible than the lighter ones outlined against the lighter surface.

So why, I've asked several plug manufacturers, doesn't someone try coloring the belly of a surface plug to contrast with the sky? I've never received a satisfactory answer and will probably have to do my own experimenting. Since the coloring on surface plugs is on the top where the fish never sees it, I can only assume it was put there more to attract fishermen than fish.

Underwater plugs use the same color scheme, colored on the top and sides and fish belly white on the bottom. But here it might make more sense because the predator is getting a three-dimensional view. Maybe if I were to reverse this pattern to give the gamefish easier visibility. . .

Scientists tell us, incidentally, that red and yellow are the colors most visible to fish. I know of no red and yellow baitfish common along the North Atlantic Coast. Yet on several occasions a fluorescent red swimming plug caught stripers and blues for me when other colors failed.

Unfortunately a theory that is backed with no other evidence than personal experience and observation is bound to be open to contradiction. Why will gamefish attack a plug with exotic coloring that is foreign to their environment? My explanation is simply that in cases where fish strike unnatural colors, visibility rather than conformity may be the governing factor.

Going back again to my fresh water bassing days, there is no question in my mind that the higher visibility of the black surface plugs made them more effective. Nature provides frogs, which many plugs represent, with white bellies, so the black undersides certainly were not what the large-mouth bass were accustomed to seeing. Yet they went for them.

Gamefish do recognize color and will respond to certain colors at certain times. This is well established. There are times when gamefish will take only one color pattern of otherwise identical lures. So the answer seems to be that fish, at times, prefer one color over another. Visibility may sometimes be a more important factor than environmental considerations.

One other point on the color of plugs. I have successfully used the kids' crayons to color plugs. The crayon coating endures and has the added advantage of being removable.

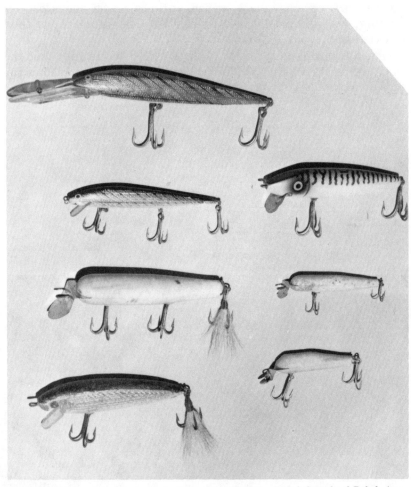

Swimming Plugs: Left row, top to bottom—Deep Running Rebel, Standard Rebel, Atom Junior, Atom Reactor.

Right Row, top to bottom—Point Jude Cutlass, Atom Swimmer, Atom Coho.

The element that makes a swimming plug act the way it does, or is supposed to, is the wobble plate or face plate—the metal or plastic arrangement set in the nose. Its design, size, and placement determine the action. Those factors, plus the placement of the pull rung determines how deep it will run.

Almost all swimming plugs, even the deep runners, float when at rest. Thus when they are retrieved they dig down into the water where the resistance sets them in motion.

In the accompanying picture the Deep Running Rebel, upper left, has an elongated plastic bill-like wobble plate with the pull ring located about half way along. Pulling this plug through the water forces the nose down, and it will wriggle its way into the lower levels.

Directly below that, for comparison, is a standard Rebel. It has similar body contours, but the smaller wobble plate and the location of the pull ring directly on the nose means this plug will swim just under the surface with a quick, side-to-side motion.

The Atom Junior, pictured next below, has a larger wobble plate and the pull ring is set below the center. When retrieved slowly this plug will laze along the surface. More speed will bring it just under the surface. Bend the pull ring up and it will go deeper. The wide wobble plate gives it an exaggerated swimming motion at any speed.

The Point Jude Cutlass, upper right, and the Atom Reactor, lower left, both have mid-sized wobble plates set low and the pull ring directly in front which will cause them to swim a little below the surface with a wobbling action somewhere between that of the standard Rebel and the Atom Junior.

The Coho, lower right, has a large wobble plate slanted somewhat toward the horizontal while the small Atom swimmer above it has a smaller wobble plate bent toward the vertical. The difference causes the Coho to have an exaggerated wobble, while the swimmer has a slower action. The manufacturer's instructions are built around the plug's design and its intended action.

Underwater plugs come designed to deliver all sorts of wobbles, shakes, twitches, weaving motions, dives, shimmies, wriggles, contortions and what-have-you. Most come with instructions on how best to take advantage of said wobbles, shakes, etc. You can create all sorts of motion by working the rod tip and/or varying the speed. If you don't have any luck following the instructions, try experimenting.

But don't be fooled into thinking you've solved a problem if your experiment pays off. Because tomorrow the preferences of the fish may require that you change back to your original system as per the instructions. Stay flexible and don't be afraid to experiment.

On the other hand don't be too swift in monkeying with the plug itself. Most plug makers engineer their plugs carefully for balance and action. I know one who goes underwater with scuba gear to watch his plugs in action when testing them. Although I have not been able to determine how he knows just what action the gamefish are looking for.

Many fishermen alter their plugs by bending the pull ring up to make them run deeper, or down to make them run closer to the surface. Little harm is done to the action and the plug may be reaching a more productive level.

But major surgery is often tricky. Bending the lip or wobble plate will alter its intended action, possibly for the better, but more likely for the worse. You may destroy the plug's effectiveness. Changing hooks is dangerous unless the substitute hooks are the same weight as the original.

I know of one case where a fisherman was having great luck hooking blues with a particular plug, but little luck landing them. The rather thin light-wire hooks just were not holding. So he threw away the original hooks and substituted heavier ones. The added weight affected the plug's action, and it was no longer attractive to the fish. He'd have been better off going to a rod with softer action; thus reducing some of the pressure on the hooks.

As in most cases where advice is given in this book, there are cases that disprove the advice. There are times when tinkering pays off as is demonstrated in the case of the Reverse Atom. And then there was the case of Nick Mignacca and his tandem plug.

Nobody was catching any fish that October afternoon. The stripers, schooled up for the fall migration, had been in close a few times during the day, but now were nowhere to be seen. Nick had tried everything without success until he dug into the market basket he was using for a plug bag and pulled out a creation that might be called the nothing-else-works-so-let's-try-this-plug.

Nick Mignacca and the striper he caught on his tandem plug

Actually it was two plugs hitched in tandem; a swimming plug in front and a bullet-headed surface slider in the rear. Together they measured something over a foot in length and weighed perhaps a quarter of a pound. A bass would only hit a plug like that in self defense.

Those of us watching simply grinned. Desperation, we agreed, had driven Nick to the absurd. But the absurd is never very far off in surf fishing. Nick lobbed the monstrosity out. It landed with a splash like a falling watermelon. He started the retrieve. There was a swirl and he was onto a twelve pound striped bass. The grins of the onlookers were quickly erased and there was some frantic searching through tackle bags for plugs that could be rigged in tandem.

I took Nick's picture holding the fish—the only one caught that afternoon along that section of shoreline.

Another word of warning: Don't try to save money by buying cheaper imitations of standard lures. They may look exactly the same, but they're not. A number of firms, both foreign and domestic, are producing cheap imitations of the Rapala and Rebel plugs. The hardware isn't as reliable, the workmanship is shoddy, and the plugs just don't perform as well as the originals.

And don't buy a plug because it has the exact color and configuration of a baitfish. When the easily-molded plastics appeared some lure makers took advantage of the new material to create lures that could almost pass for the real thing. They had scale markings, fins, gill covers, everything. I've got a mackerel plug from that era so realistic I've been tempted to fillet it more than once. Yet it has never caught a fish. It just doesn't have the action.

After a while the manufacturers went back to making plugs that suggested, rather than duplicated, the original. They were more successful by far. I believe this has to do with the vibrations sent out by the movements of a real fish. Marine predators, as mentioned earlier, use this ability to pick up vibrations to find their prey. They follow their sonar to the prey and then strike, not waiting to check the proper number of stripes or if the fin placement is just right.

These exact duplicate lures had all the exact markings, but they weren't acting like real fish. As my kids would say, they had bad vibes. So they didn't work. Gamefish aren't interested in anything that doesn't send out the right impulses.

Scientists also keep coming up with ideas that will help us catch fish. Some years ago some researcher found that human hands have a trace of a chemical that repels fish. Strangely enough, it is present in a much larger degree in men than in women.

This chemical rubs off on your lures when you're handling them. Tests proved this. And the chemical is easily detected by fish. Some fresh water bass fishermen carry soap to wash their hands before they handle their lures, and I know one shad fisherman who always washed his hands with toothpaste before touching his shad darts. The fact that this shad fisherman consistently outfished everyone on the river was not lost on me.

Several years ago we were cleaning out the family car at the end of the summer and my wife found a well-squeezed tube of toothpaste in the glove compartment. She asked me what it was doing there. I replied, "You wouldn't believe it if I told you." All right, fishermen have been catching fish for centuries without washing their hands. But most of us need all the edge we can get. Wash your hands before handling your plugs. If it doesn't do anything else, you'll have clean hands.

And while we're on the subject of smell, stink plugs have had their day and are still seen occasionally. These were plugs that were designed to be treated with a scent, usually by injecting fish oil or some other material in a small reservoir. The substance would leak out gradually and form a chum line that would lead the gamefish to the plug.

I can recall sitting on the tailgate of a station wagon laboriously injecting the oil from a can of sardines into a small hole in a plug with a medicine dropper, and then, of course, eating the sardines. I can't recall that this did any more than make my plug bag smell worse than usual. The stink plugs were gimmicks, and gimmicks don't catch fish.

Some fresh water plugs work well on small surf gamesters. If you're going to use them, it's a good idea to replace the original hooks with barbs made to last in salt water. When small blues, stripers, and weaks are feeding on small bait, these lures can be killers.

New plugs will have appeared on the market by the time this book reaches the store shelf. Some of them will be along traditional lines; some will depart from tradition. There probably won't be any new concepts in design, except for new materials and finishes. We've not seen the end of new plug designs necessarily, but there has to be a limit to what game fish are willing to accept as something edible.

The basic function of a plug is to represent a bait fish. Design must be limited to those representations. No matter what the design, the basic principles of use as outlined in this chapter will apply. No plug will catch fish under all circumstances.

DROPPERS AND TRAILERS

Long ago when the only plugs available were those designed to be cast with the big surf rigs, imaginative surf fishermen devised a way to take some of the smaller gamesters. They ran droppers about three feet ahead of their plugs. These droppers were often simple white bucktails or strips of pork rind, but they picked up school size bass and blues that would be intimidated by the huge plugs. I have sometimes wondered if the fish thought these droppers were small baitfish being pursued by larger fish. Maybe they did. At any rate, they worked.

And they still work, although now we have light spinning tackle that will cast lures of suitable size to take these smaller fish. The droppers remain a valuable tool for those who use heavy tackle for big fish, but would like a few frying pan size stripers as well.

The trailers were usually bucktails that were streamed a yard or so in back of a metal jig. Years ago we tied up some red and white bucktails on tandem hooks that were murder on school bass when trailed behind a jig.

The late Jerry Sylvester of Narragansett is credited with inventing the broomhandle rig which consisted of a section of broomhandle which served as a casting weight with a small, bucktail jig trailing behind. I suspect this arrangement was not original with Sylvester. Jersey fishermen, who don't miss many bets, were using it on weakfish long before Jerry was around. Southern New England fishermen found this rig to be particularly effective for the pollock that come inshore in early winter to feed on small fish. Now those fishermen, like everybody else, have spinning rigs that will cast the bucktails without the broomhandles.

Here are some more odds and ends about plugging that may be of value:

Beware of plugs whose hooks are mounted too close together. They too often tangle during the cast, thus destroying the plug's action on the retrieve. There is nothing more maddening than stopping to untangle hooks every other cast. If you have a plug with this built-in trait, substitute hooks with shorter shanks. If that fails, take off one hook entirely. If that ruins the plug's action, throw the damned thing away and write a nasty letter to the manufacturer.

Look for plugs that are wired through. On these plugs the pull ring to which you hitch your line or leader runs through the plug to the tail hook. Any hooks in between are hung from the center wire. Few fish can dismantle a plug that is wired through, but they can, and do, twist out hooks mounted on screw eyes. However, don't let screw eyes keep you from a plug that catches fish. The screw eyes hold under normal pressures.

The less hardware you carry on the end of your line the better your plug action will be, particularly with swimming plugs. For that reason I never use wire leaders on plugs even when fishing for bluefish which have a notorious reputation for their ability to slice a monofiliment or braided line with their teeth.

The fact is when a blue is hooked on a plug its teeth are rarely in a position to reach the line. Sure, another blue can come along and snap at your snap or swivel and cut you off, but that's even more likely to happen if the snap or swivel is a foot away at the end of a wire leader.

Actually, tying your line directly to the plug gives the plug maximum freedom of action, but this makes changing plugs a tiresome job—especially at night. So I compromise by using a snap, the smallest one practical, but no swivel. Since a plug does not spin in the water you have no use for a swivel anyway. A black snap will discourage attacks by blues which will often, when in a feeding frenzy, slash at anything that glitters or shines.

I like a bucktail on a surface popper, but not on a swimmer. Dancing behind a surface popper, the bucktail on the swinging tail hook provides a little extra inducement. But it does very little except deaden the action of a swimming plug, especially one of those slowly-weaving swimmers you want to use on a dark, still night. You know what picking up a weed on the tail hook does to the action of your swimming plug. Well, a bucktail does the same thing. I suspect manufacturers put bucktails on the tail hooks of swimming plugs because it makes them more attractive to buyers.

In choosing a plug for any situation, look first to the size of the bait the gamefish are chasing. While fish may be careless about such details as color, they will often be choosy about size. If a school of stripers is into a school of two-inch long silversides, they're much more likely to hit a lure of comparable size. If your rig is too heavy to cast a two-inch lure, go to the dropper I mentioned above.

Color can be important if the fish are feeding selectively. Many marine baitfish have silvery or bluish hues. Plugs painted in those colors seem to have universal success. If you can find out what the fish are feeding on, it might help to use a plug with coloration matching the bait.

When stripers or bluefish, particularly bluefish, are in a feeding frenzy, hardly anything matters except that you get a lure of some kind into the melee as soon as possible. Even when tearing into a school of bait, stripers will sometimes limit their attacks to plugs of the general size and appearance of the bait they're chasing. Bluefish, on the other hand, will hit anything that moves.

To prove this point Tom Morrison and I once rigged bucktail hooks on a spark plug, a beer can opener, a closet door handle, a fountain pen, a clothes pin and a potato peeler. We cast them into a school of feeding blues off Prudence Island in Narragansett Bay and caught fish on every one of them.

What usually happens to plug fishermen is that they find a half dozen or so plugs that work well. These are the ones that find permanent berths in the surf bag. Just what plugs they are depends on where you fish and what you fish for. Sometimes selections even change with the seasons. Plug fishermen occasionally try new plugs and once in a while even adopt one, which may replace a former favorite. But most of the time the same battered and tooth-marked plugs will remain.

METAL JIGS

There are other ways of catching fish besides plugging, and we will now consider metal jigs. Metal jigs pre-date plugs by a good many years. Before plugs were widely merchandised, they were the most commonly used artificial lures. Today's metal lures are somewhat different from those earlier ones, and they are probably as effective. You'll still hear many an old gaffer with a thumb grooved from years of guiding Cuttyhunk or braided nylon onto a revolving spool reel tell you nothing can compare with the old block tin squid.

There's not much block tin around any more. Most of today's metal lures are cast in one of several alloys and coated with chrome or some other shining material, but squidding with block tin is not a lost art by any means. Let's take a look at it.

The lures were pure tin — a metal that produces a soft, translucent glow that is not duplicated in the finishes of today's metal lures. While that sheen would fade after the lure was exposed to the salt water, it could be quickly restored with a little steel wool, fine emory cloth, or even by rubbing it in the sand. The traditional block tin squid were about four inches long, flat on top, and keeled along the bottom. They carried a single tail hook dressed with either feathers or bucktail, with white feathers preferred by most. They weighed in somewhere between one and two ounces. There was no real standard since many tackle dealers poured their own, as did quite a few fishermen (who still do, by the way).

You could also get them poured in lead. These were less expensive, but the lead was a poor substitute for tin. Lead discolors quickly and is not as easily polished. Its weight takes away some of the action found in pure tin.

Since the design of these lures has always been a somewhat free-hand art form, varieties in shape and size are many. Each tackle store that makes them, as well as each fisherman who has a melting pot in his cellar and a mold, has his own idea of the best design. Depending on the design and the speed of the retrieve, they can be made to wobble seductively or dart from side to side. A little work with the rod tip can send them into all sorts of appealing motions.

They cast like bullets, being compact and streamlined. One year in November when fishing from the rocks at Narragansett, one of the last schools of migrating bass was cavorting just beyond casting range of the few die-hard fishermen who were still with it that late in the season. Our plugs just wouldn't reach the school. I dug out a 25 year old block tin squid I had rubbed down the night before. It caught four before the school moved on.

As the price of tin soared after the war and more and more plugs appeared on the market, block tin squid became less popular. Nevertheless, people continue to make them, and there will always be surf fishermen to use them.

Today's metal lures are more likely to be in the style of the Hopkins

Lure, a hammered metal lure shaped roughly like the handle of a jackknife—or the Kastmaster, a flat piece of metal with a swinging hook. There are many variations of both.

Metal lures have several advantages over plugs. They are more compact and will cast farther. The flash they throw off from their chrome, stainless, or tin sides attracts gamefish. They can be fished deep if the prey happens to be hugging the bottom or they can be retrieved close to the surface. Virtually any predator fish will take them, and they are made in sizes to attract any gamefish from cow bass and slammer blues down to fluke and weakfish.

Metal spoons have never been counted as primary weapons by surf casters, although they are used at times. Their major fault is that they cast poorly. They tend to sail rather than drill through the air, costing the caster both distance and accuracy. Trollers will testify that they are among the deadliest of lures.

Traditionally, metal is for daytime use only. I have already mentioned that night when block tin squid took stripers for me from the north jetty of the Shark River Inlet in North Jersey and metal has scored for me on other moonlit nights as well. But they are primarily used during daylight hours.

Tom Morrison and I often experiment and tinker with lures. We once painted some tin with phosphorescent paint on the theory that the pale blue glow would attract gamefish at night. It didn't. Not a one. But we found that in the half light of early dawn or on heavily overcast days they were more effective than unpainted lures.

Squidding, to give metal lure fishing its traditional name, is something more demanding than plug fishing, although the two are closely related. Both plugs and tin squid have built in action, but it requires more on the part of the fisherman to get the action out of tin.

The time to use metal, whether it's the old, block tin squid or one of the more modern manifestations, is when an onshore wind is kicking up the surf. Now schools of bait will be broken up and the bait tumbled in the churning water. Your lure should land out beyond the line of breakers, just behind a breaking wave. As the wave charges shoreward your lure will follow in the turbulence where predators are waiting to grab the disoriented bait.

Where white water is found around the ends of jetties or where rocks shove their heads through the surface to be wreathed in foam are other prime targets for the squidder. Here again is turbulent water to tumble the bait and make it easy prey for gamefish. A metal lure fluttering through this turbulence is very likely to be hit.

Tide rips, the happy and productive hunting ground for many predators, should get a look at your metal. Use a heavy lure, one that will not be swept away or tossed about too much by the tide. Make it flutter through the rip like a small fish struggling to keep its equilibrium in the turbulent water.

If your beach has an offshore bar with deep water between it and the beach, cast your lure as close to the bar as possible. Let it sink into the deep water and then retrieve at a speed that will cause it to wobble slowly near the bottom. If fish are chasing bait on the surface and breaking water, just get your lure out there and reel as fast as you can. Brace yourself.

There is one design, the sand eel squid, that is not often seen on the beaches today but once was a popular and effective lure. These are long and narrow lures, usually bent into a wavy profile and carrying a fixed rather than a swinging hook. The hook is positioned to ride point up.

These lures were useful when lures fished in the upper levels of the water failed to produce. They were retrieved slowly along the sandy bottom where they simulated a slowly-moving sand eel (which is not an eel at all, but an elongated silvery fish, common in the surf). Stripers, blues, weaks and fluke have been taken in this manner when other methods failed.

Begin your retrieve as soon as the lure hits the water just like with surface plugs. Sooner, in fact. Just take care not to try to stop the flight of your metal lure before it loses its momentum. Reel gears have been stripped in this manner, lines have popped, and rods have been torn from fingers. Wait until the lure is dropping to the water before turning the reel handle.

PURCHASING TIPS

Since many tackle stores make their own metal lures there can be wide variances in quality and workmanship. Here are tips if you're buying one:

If it's advertised as block tin, test it by biting down on it. Tin will produce a faint, crunching sound. Otherwise it's lead or some alloy.

The hole for attaching the lure to your line should be centered precisely and should be no further than 3/16 of an inch from the end. Further in makes it difficult to attach to a snap. The best lures wear brass or stainless grommets in the hole to prevent wear.

A split ring through the hole facilitates hitching and gives the lure a little more freedom of action. If the lure doesn't have one, you can attach one easily enough or you can use a large snap swivel.

In those metal lures with a fixed hook, the hook is inserted in the mold and the metal poured around it. The hook should be straight on the center line. Otherwise the lure will ride at an angle. Maybe it will catch more fish that way, but it OUGHT to be straight anyway.

Shows sloppy workmanship otherwise.

Swinging hooks, often treble on modern lures and usually dressed with feathers or bucktail, are attached to a brass wire set into the rear of the lure. The tail hook should be free and unrestricted.

BUCKTAIL JIGS

There is another type of lure that should be included in every tackle bag—a bull-headed jig, also called a bucktail jig, bug eye or barracuda. It's no more than a heavy lead head poured around a hook with bucktail or some synthetic fiber for a tail.

If I had to make a choice of a single lure to use under any and all circumstances, I'd take a bucktail jig. It is so versatile that it can be fished day or night, shallow or deep, and will take just about any gamefish that swims. The bucktail jig will often take fish when other lures fail.

I have caught more stripers (up to 32 pounds) on a bucktail jig than on any other lure, and I use them almost exclusively on weakfish. It is my favorite lure for fluke when sweetened with a strip of fish belly. When bluefish are feeling peevish, a bucktail jig will sometimes enliven their interest quicker than anything you can throw at them. The list goes on—mackerel, pollock, bonito, cod, dogfish, skate, sea robins and sand dabs as well as a variety of fresh water fish have been caught on these versatile lures.

The virtues of a bucktail jig are endless. Because it rides with the hook up it catches on bottom obstructions less than other lures. With a single, fixed hook a fish rarely succeeds in throwing or twisting it from its mouth. A fish can much more easily throw a treble hook.

Furthermore they are relatively inexpensive. A bucktail jig costs about a third as much, or less than a good salt water plug. Or you can invest in a mold and make your own for less than a quarter apiece—including the cost of the bucktail and hook.

In the larger sizes, lures such as the Smilin' Bill, the No Alibi and the original Barracuda are the prototypes; duplicated by dozens of lesser-known, but equally effective models. In the smaller sizes, the type pioneered by the Upperman jig is incomparable. The deep-bodied Upperman sinks quickly for deep-hanging gamefish. Models with flat heads plane closer to the surface. Bullet-headed styles can be worked at any level.

Selection of bucktail jigs. At the far left is a lead head equipped with a plastic grub. The next two on the top left are home-made. Note how sparse the bucktail is tied.

Some manufacturers have gone to synthetic material for the tail because of the price and scarcity of good bucktails. As a traditionalist I deplore this, even though I recognize the economic reality of the situation. I just don't believe a synthetic "breathes" the same as natural fiber. This "breathing" creates the vibrations that first lead gamefish to the lure.

Bucktail jigs impose a discipline on the angler. Where a plug or a metal lure has built-in action, a bucktail jig has none. It comes straight through the water without wriggle, wobble, or weave. Therefore it must be manipulated with the rod tip. A stiff, fast-action rod tip is recommended for the same reason this type of tip action is recommended for popping plugs—the response is quicker.

The rod tip can be made to help the jig bounce bottom, kicking up puffs of sand as it is retrieved. I know a highly successful Cape Cod angler who insists this method is the deadliest of all. Just don't try it on a rocky bottom. Even though a bucktail jig rides with the hook up, it is easily wedged in the rocks.

Twenty-five years ago I underwent a frustrating season trying to catch school stripers in the narrow gap in Coles River, Swansea, Mass., where a railroad bridge crossed the river before the 1938 hurricane took it away. Other fishermen using the same Upperman-type bucktail jigs were scoring, but I wasn't.

The following season I tasted success on my very first trip and rarely failed to score after that. During the first year I was buying my jigs at a tackle store for about 65 cents apiece and in order to protect my investments I was carefully keeping them away from the bottom of the gap which was floored with the remains of the old railroad bridge. During the winter months I got my own mold and poured my own jigs. Since I wasn't worried so much by the loss of a few jigs, I was able to jig them deep. Dozens are still hanging on the debris on the bottom of the river that second year, but I caught stripers.

I learned a few things, too. One is that the commercially tied bucktail jigs invariably wear too much hair. I tie mine with perhaps half as much bucktail as you will find on a commercial jig. If you tie your own, use the hair at the end of the bucktail. It is finer, more flexible, and breathes better than the coarser hair found at the base of the tail.

As for colors, a red and white head seems universally popular. I've also experimented with yellow combined with either red or white and that seems to work as well. Some chrome-plated jigs have also been successful. White tails are as effective as any, although I like to add a thin strand of color down each side.

I have tied in such added attractors as a lock of hair from the head of a blond daughter, a few strands of hair from a collie, and some electric blue nylon hair from a doll to dress a bucktail jig. I can't say they helped; but they didn't hurt either.

Except for my domestic situation. When my wife learned I had clipped a few strands of hair from my daughter I was given clear notice that this would be the last time. The consequences were not spelled out and I didn't care to make a test case of it. The matter of the doll with the electric blue nylon hair resulted in financial loss.

Many marine baitfish have a bluish tinge along the side and back, and I had never found a suitable shade to mix with my white bucktail. The doll's hair looked excellent.

I graciously opened negotiations with the 5-year-old owner with an offer of an ice cream cone. She started at two dollars. I went to a hot fudge sundae. She stuck with her original position. I told the little thief she was an ungrateful child and broke off the bargaining talks. Two dollars indeed. The whole doll probably wasn't worth more than a dollar. And anyway, I knew she'd get tired of playing with it in a day or so and I could scoff it up and away to my cellar retreat. Which is just what happened.

No five-year-old, I told myself, was going to get the best of me. I had just started tying when the little bounder sneaked down the cellar stairs, saw the shorn doll lying on the bench, and set up a howl. This time there was no bargaining. It was two bucks and an ice cream cone or tell Mother. I ponied up, being well aware of Mother's attitude toward the pirating of dolls for tying bucktail jigs.

Another little trick. Tie a strip of gold or silver Mylar along each flank. I've never seen them tied commercially that way, but I've had some outstanding successes with it.

The bucktail jig is the most versatile of lures, but is probably the most effective when the fish are deep. Weakfish particularly like them when they are bounced along the bottom and bottom-dwelling fluke are also partial to lures fished in this manner. With stripers and blues, just find the depth they're at and fish accordingly.

Many fishermen, and I'm one of them, like a strip of pork rind on the hook for added appeal. It's a deadly combination, but perhaps more deadly is a strip of fish belly. If fluke are present you can't miss with a bucktail jig decorated with a strip of fluke belly. Cut the strip long and thin so it will have a little flutter to it. A strip of squid is also effective. Some dress the hook with a bit of shrimp when after weakfish, clam when after stripers, or sea worm when after most anything.

Lead-headed jigs can also be dressed with plastic skirts, and plastic worms can be added. These are growing in popularity, especially among those who seek weakfish. The so-called grub, a flap-tailed, round-bellied elongated hunk of plastic, can be slipped onto the bare hook of a lead head to make an effective weakfish lure. These grubs are not widely used in southern New England, although they are available in some stores. Two years ago I picked up a dozen in various colors (they're only a dime each), brought them back north, and tried them on Narragansett Bay weakfish. They outfished the bucktail jigs my companions were using.

Another version are the Spiral Tails, introduced about a year ago. These, too, can be killers.

One last word on bucktail jigs—when you fish them, jig them. Keep your rod tip jumping.

ARTIFICIAL BAIT

Another group of artificial lures bears mentioning in this section, although they are not widely used in surf fishing. These are the artificial worms, eels, and squid—invariably soft plastic or rubber lures that are fish killers at times, but difficult to cast for the most part. They are widely used by boat fishermen.

Probably the most popular lure of this type is the artificial eel of which the Alou Eel is one of the oldest and best known. A molded metal head gives it weight, and a wobble plate set in the head gives it action. These lures come in several sizes and colors, with black the most popular shade. These lures are fished along the bottom with just enough speed to give them action. Their main disadvantage is their bulk-weight ratio which makes them awkward to cast. They have a nasty habit of hanging the tail hooks around the head during a cast.

The same applies to surgical tubing lures—highly successful trolling rigs, but difficult to cast. It has never been clear to me whether these lures, which are sometimes 18 inches or more in length, represent a long sea worm or a thin eel. Whatever it is, stripers and blues are partial to them. Trollers working Horseshoe Shoal off Cape Cod use tubing lures two feet long for bluefish. I'd hate to try to cast one of those.

Artificial squid have never been particular favorites of surf fishermen. These generally have lead heads enclosed in plastic with long, fringed skirts. A while back the Hootchie Troll hit the market and literally slaughtered stripers and blues around Cape Cod. Some surf fishermen tried them, but they were not suited to surf casting.

Section 3

Bottom Rigs and Bait

I wasn't fishing that evening, just walking the beach and enjoying the long, June twilight. There wasn't much moving on the outer Cape Cod waters anyway. A week earlier some school stripers had moved into Head of The Meadow Beach in Truro where I was camped, but they seemed to have moved off. There were reportedly some bass at Race Point, but I didn't have a beach buggy so the race was out of my reach. It was a little early for bluefish in these waters.

The lone fisherman on the beach was standing by his sand-spiked rod picking through the seaweed in a box such as those used to carry sea worms. He looked up when I approached.

"I got one more worm," he said, "I'm gonna feed that to the crabs and then, by God, I'm goin' back to Chicopee an' spend the rest of my life fishin' in fresh water."

"No luck, huh?"

"Luck," he said, "You want to talk about luck? Let me tell you about luck. I left Chicopee at 1 o'clock this mornin' and drove all night. Stopped at a bait shop in Buzzard's Bay and asked the guy what the fish were hittin'. I only get down for surf fishin' a couple of times a year, you see, and this guy generally gives me pretty good advice."

He rummaged in his bag and drew out a plug, one that was popular that year on the Cape. "He sold me this. Said if anything would catch a fish this would. Told me there were some fish along here."

"He wasn't lying," I said. "We had school bass along here until a few days ago, but most of them seem to have moved out. Could be a few around, though."

"Oh, yeah, there's a few around, I seen a couple of them. You see that bar out there? When I got here this afternoon the bar was covered. See just to the right? There's a cut there. Good, deep cut for the fish to get through inside the bar. Everything looked good. Pretty fair ground swell to kick up some white water, just a little offshore breeze, even saw some bait flashin' in the water just off the wash."

I commented, "Sounds good."

He agreed. "Yeah, sounds good. I started pluggin' usin' this here plug. Looked great in the water. Plugged for an hour. Tried poppers, swimmers, metal, nuthin' doin'. Then an hour or so ago this fat dude came along with his fat wife who was dressed in one o' them mumus and a fat little kid, one of the nastiest lookin' kids I ever saw. They got a couple of fresh water rods and some clam worms. They want to know what's bitin' and I tell 'em nuthin'. They ain't nuthin' bitin'. But they're goin' to try it anyway. So they bait up with the worms and cast out and the first thing you know the kid has a strike an' what does she do but haul out a nice schoolie, maybe three or four pounds. Then the fat broad does the same thing. And they only been here about 15 minutes.

"The guy wants to know what kind of fish they are and if they're good to eat. I tell him they're stripers and they're good to eat. Then he wants to know how to cook 'em. I'm gettin' steamed now, so I tell him the only way to cook striped bass is to roast 'em on a spit over an open fire, figurin' he's stayin' at the campground where they don't allow no open fires, the jerk.

"They start off the beach and I ask him if I can buy the worms he's got left over, but he says no. He thinks he'll keep 'em in case they like the striped bass. They might want to catch some more tomorrow, he says.

"So I pack up my gear, drive 'way the hell to Provincetown to get a couple of dozen worms, drive back here and start fishin'. Only by now the tide's dropped, the bar's outta water an' all I been doin' is feedin' crabs on worms that cost me a dime apiece."

When I left he was making his final cast with his final worm and when I returned from my walk only the empty worm box marked the spot. He was on his way back to Chicopee where, presumably, the gods of fishing luck are kinder.

The story illustrates an all-important point. A fisherman using bait often has the advantage over the fisherman who is trying to convince the fish that a hunk of plastic would be just the thing for an afternoon snack.

I take no position in the traditional and continuing debate over whether bait or artificials is the more effective and/or sporting way to take gamefish from the surf. My practice is to use whatever is at hand and which seems to have the most promise in any given situation. I don't mind change when circumstances warrant it.

I haven't seen any statistics on it, but I suspect there are many more fish hauled from the surf on baited hooks than from artificial lures. Many ocean fish are simply not the least bit interested in artificials. I've never heard of a tautog or a kingfish being taken on an artificial, for instance, and while fluke will accept a bucktail jig as good, honest meat, most are taken on bait.

Moreover, those surf fishermen addicted exclusively to hardware are in the minority. The traditional, outdoor magazine image of a surf fisherman is a dude wearing waders and parka, a surf bag on his shoulder, a gaff and knife at his belt and a three dollar and fifty cent plug hanging from his rod tip. But for every one of these there are a hundred others in sneakers and dungarees casting baits from jetties and beaches, and another dozen surf-wise old bait soakers sitting on beach chairs, their rods propped in sand spikes and fish buried in the sand behind them.

A successful bait fisherman requires the same knowledge of the surf and its inhabitants as the plug fisherman. Each studies the movements of the bait and predators, examines the stomach contents of fish, calculates the effects of season, tide, wind, weather and time of day, to come up with a fairly good idea of what bait or lure to use. And each must learn how to present his offering for maximum results.

Yet too many bait fishermen simply find a convenient spot along the shore or on a jetty, bait up and heave, hoping for something to come along.

That's not the way to do it. Success with this approach can be attributed to pure, dumb luck. While luck can happen to anybody; it happens mostly to those who help it along.

The wise bait fisherman, first of all, selects his bait carefully. He wants it fresh in most cases, although there are times when a certain ripeness adds to the charm of a piece of bait. If he's fishing live bait he wants it to be lively and takes measures to keep it fresh and lively while transporting it. His terminal tackle will be designed to present the bait in the most natural manner and to permit him to have the most sensitive connection with it. His hooks will be of a design appropriate to the task, and they will be needle sharp. He will not cast blindly into the sea, but will place his bait expertly where he knows the fish are likely to be.

Bait fishing is not the haphazard activity many suppose it to be. It is an ancient and honorable pursuit requiring every bit as much expertise as working an artificial lure. Before we get into what baits are appropriate to what fish, we should take a look at bottom rigs.

BOTTOM RIGS

There are basically two types of rigs—the *fishfinder,* which permits the line to run freely through the sinker when the bait is picked up by a fish, and the *fixed sinker* rig which anchors the bait to the floor of the sea. There are countless variations of both.

Then there are the sinkers—*egg, bank, pyramid* and *flat.* Egg sinkers are ovate with a hole running through the longitudinal axis. These go on fishfinder rigs. They will not hold bottom where there is a current running laterally along the beach or where the tide is moving through an inlet. They will roll with the tide.

Bank sinkers are best on a rocky bottom. They will hang up in the rocks to be sure, but not as easily as other types. Bank sinkers are shaped generally like drops of water with the holes in the small end.

Pyramid sinkers are best suited to sandy bottoms. They will hold in a running tide better than egg or bank sinkers. They are not well suited to rocky bottoms. Their sharp corners make them prone to hangups.

Flat sinkers are designed to hold in an inlet where the tide runs swiftly. For some reason they are not in general use although they are efficient. Cape Cod Canal fishermen use them to hold bottom in the five-knot current that swirls through that ditch. If your tackle store doesn't stock them, lay a bank sinker on a rock and hammer it until it's flat. It won't be neat or pretty, but it will do the job.

Fishfinder rigs are widely used on fish that might spook and drop the bait when they feel the weight of the sinker. Fluke, school stripers, and kingfish fall in this category. Cow bass don't seem to mind carrying off a few ounces of lead. Bluefish are so intent on getting something to eat, they just don't seem to care. A tautog would carry off a sash weight and hardly notice it.

A fishfinder rig is simplicity itself. Just thread the end of your line through the eye of your sinker and tie on a barrel swivel big enough to stop the sinker from running down over the hook. To the other eye of the swivel tie your leader. Some use hangers or snaps to hang the sinker on the line. When a fish picks up the bait and runs he will be pulling the line through the sinker and will not have the weight of the sinker to cope with. And the fisherman on the other end of the line will have a better feel for what's happening at the hook end.

The fishfinder is usually, but not always, a single hook rig. Some use a high-low arrangement with two hooks, one of which is floated off the bottom with a cork.

Fixed sinker rigs use a three-way swivel at the end of the line. From one eye is a leader attached to a sinker. The other eye takes the hook leader. Multiple hook rigs are made by attaching another hook above the first in the same manner.

Where crabs or other bottom-grubbing pests are cleaning your hooks before the baitfish can find the bait, use a float close to the hook. A simple bottle cork will do the job, but many prefer the brightly-colored, cigar-shaped floats sold in every tackle store from

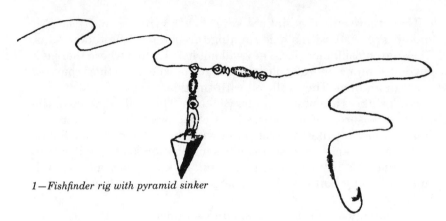

1—Fishfinder rig with pyramid sinker

2—Fishfinder rig with egg sinker

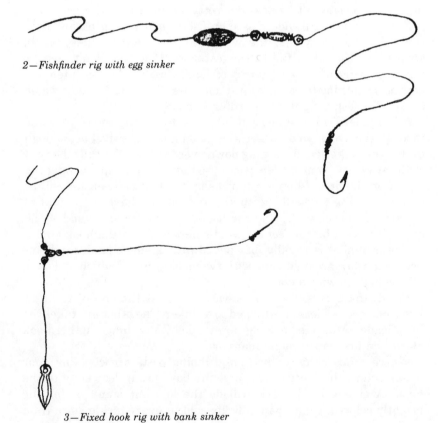

3—Fixed hook rig with bank sinker

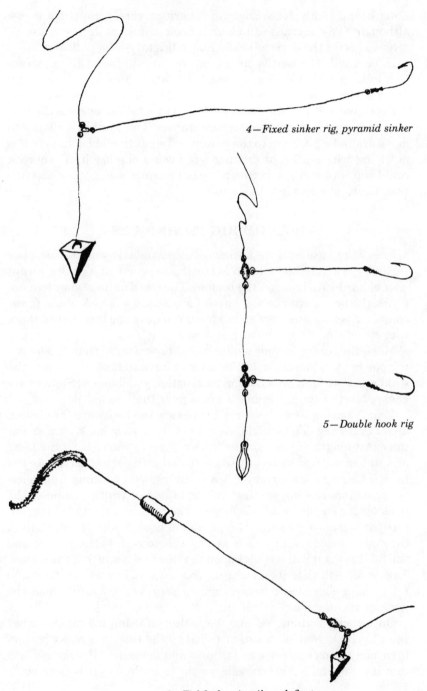

4—*Fixed sinker rig, pyramid sinker*

5—*Double hook rig*

6—*Fishfinder rig wih cork float.*

Long Island south. New England fishermen rarely use these floats, although Yankee crabs can clean a hook as fast as Jersey crabs.

Some prefer the Jersey Doodle Bug, a brightly-colored float dressed with bucktail. The bait is pinned on the built-in hook. The contraption looks a little like a pregnant fresh water bass bug. It is highly regarded by some, but I've never been able to bring myself to try one.

I'm convinced a floating bait anchored by a fishfinder rig is the best way to present it under most circumstances. The bait has a chance to move around a bit, close to the bottom where it should be and yet it is not lying where a bit of drifting weed could obscure it or where it could slip into a crack between rocks or under some other obstruction. Crabs are also less likely to find it.

BOTTOM RIG TECHNIQUES

First of all, use as little hardware as possible. If you use barrel or three-way swivels, make them as small as is practical. You don't want a lot of hardware lying on the bottom. The more natural your bait appears, the better chance you have of attracting a fish. And the fewer snaps, swivels, connectors and so forth you have the less chance there is of something letting go at the wrong time.

Make the leader to your sinker of lighter material than the leader to your hook. The sinker leader doesn't have to hold a fish, just the sinker. If that fouls on a bottom obstruction you'll lose it. Sinkers are cheap. Most of the fishermen I know pour their own. I do.

If you're using a two-hook rig, make sure the hooks are far enough apart that they don't tangle. And don't have your hook on a leader the exact length of your sinker leader. Sure as you're born the hook and sinker will find some way to get fouled with each other. Make the hook leader a little shorter for beach fishing. When fishing from a jetty for bottom-feeding species such as tautog or winter flounder, the hook leader should be a little longer. The line, when jetty fishing, enters the water at a sharper angle. If the hook leader is longer than the sinker leader, your bait is more likely to rest on the bottom and the fish taking it will be tugging on the line and not lifting the sinker. This is for fish that feed right on the bottom. For weaks, bass and fluke, all of which seek free-swimming prey, you can either float the hook or tie on a shorter leader.

On a rocky bottom you may be better off using too much rather than too little weight. A sinker rolled by the tide on a rocky bottom invariably finds a crevice to fall into and get stuck. If your rod will cast it comfortably, use enough weight to anchor your bottom rig.

There is one drawback to a heavy sinker. It gives the fish more leverage in its efforts to escape. There must be a compromise. Your sinker should be heavy enough to hold bottom, particularly among the rock, but no heavier than necessary.

On a sand bottom it doesn't matter much if your sinker moves a little with the tide. In fact it might help to have a little movement as long as it isn't swept back to shore downtide.

And it isn't always necessary to have regular sinkers, by the way. Nuts and bolts and other odds and ends of metal have served in an emergency; as have rocks, which were probably history's first sinkers. Some folks simply tie small bags of sand and use them.

HOOKS

Dull hooks probably lose more fish than anything else. We've all seen fishermen cursing bait-stealing fish. They feel a bite, yank, feel the fish on briefly, and then lose it. Some of this may be because they are trying to set the hook too soon or are waiting until it is too late. Often the hook isn't sharp enough to get a good bite into flesh. A hook hone or a small point file should be kept in the tackle box or surf bag.

I'm not going to suggest specific hook styles and sizes for surf fishing except in a very general way. If in doubt, go to a slightly smaller size rather than to a larger one. It seems to me that it's easier to sink say, a 1/0 hook into the mouth of almost any fish than a 3/0, even if the fish has a mouth big enough to accommodate the 3/0.

There are regional preferences in style and size. A Cape Cod fisherman might thread three or four worms on a 3/0 to 4/0 O'Shaughnessy for stripers while a New Jersey fisherman would probably stream a single worm from a smaller, lighter hook. Tautog have leathery mouths so tautog fishermen everywhere lean to short, stout hooks while those fishing for weakfish, which have tender mouths, use long shanked light wire hooks. Winter flounder with tiny mouths call for hooks with tiny bends such as the Chestertown.

Bait holder hooks such as the Eagle Claw are favored by many, especially for soft baits such as worms or clams. They don't prevent bait stealing, but they do make it a little more difficult. And they hold the bait better, preventing it from slipping down the shank and bunching at the bend.

The type of bait being used is another factor governing the selection of a hook size. Grass shrimp, for instance, require a fine wire hook no matter what the gamefish you're seeking. If the main course of your intended fish dinner is something that will be enticed only by a golfball-sized hunk of clam or a slab of butterfish, your hook will have to be big enough to accommodate it.

Use quality hooks. They're not all that expensive.

Tie up some extra rigs before you go fishing, particularly if you'll be fishing where there are rocks or other bottom obstructions. Making them up on your work bench is easier than making them up on the beach. If you run out of rigs you can make do with a simple arrangement you can whip together in a few minutes. Simply tie a loop in the end of your line and hang the sinker on it. Then make another loop at an appropriate distance above and hitch your hook to that. You can tie on a second hook the same way for a two-hook rig. These jury-rigged arrangements are fine for smaller fish such as kings or weaks or small bass and blues, but they are not as reliable for larger fish. The loop knots are not as strong as the knots you would use on swivels.

Some anglers rig for weaks and fluke by tying on a cigar-shaped trolling sinker and streaming the hook a couple of feet behind. When using this rig the idea is to cast and then retrieve slowly along the bottom. It is effective for that purpose, but is appropriate for this method only. The sinker will roll along the bottom during ordinary bottom fishing and very likely cause your terminal tackle to foul itself. If a fish picks it up, he will be picking up the weight of the sinker.

I dislike wire leaders. They are difficult to work with and are highly visible to the fish. As stated in the last section I don't use them with artificial lures and have never lost a bluefish.

But bait fishing is different. A blue ingesting a hunk of cut bait may get it deep enough so his teeth can close on the line or leader. If that happens, the fish is gone. When bluefish are present the safest bet is to rig your hooks on short wire leaders.

BAIT FISHING

For one type of bait fishing no sinker at all or only a small clamp-on is needed. Stripers and blues are caught in many places by live-lining live bait such as eels, bunker or herring. Grass shrimp and worms are sometimes live-lined for weakfish or bass.

This technique usually involves a falling tide at an inlet or river mouth. The live bait, hooked in a way that will keep it alive and swimming in a natural manner, is cast into the current and permitted to drift freely down the tide. In the Cape Cod Canal early spring striper fishermen hook their herring lightly in front of the dorsal fin, cast them into the current, and walk them along the bank, keeping pace with the current. Night tides at the Charlestown Beachway in

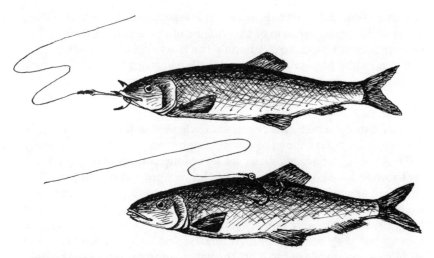

Whole baitfish can be hooked through the lips or the back, just in front of the dorsal fin, for live bait fishing.

Rhode Island find the short East Jetty populated with a tight knot of fishermen floating live eels down the tide while competing for space to stand. Some try live-line eels or bunker from the beach.

Terminal tackle for this technique is simplicity itself. A short leader (wire if blues are around) usually of heavier test than the line, holds the hook. Some simply tie the hook on the end of the line. In fast flowing water a small clamp-on sinker is sometimes used to bring the bait down to where the fish are feeding.

Tackle for bait fishing will vary with the size of the fish sought, the type of bait being used, and the nature of the area being fished. For much bait fishing, spinning tackle does the job. But where sinkers of more than three ounces are used, standard surf rods and reels are called for. Even if the prey is small—school stripers, kings, weaks, small blues—it is often necessary to go to full size surf spinning tackle to deliver the bait to the feeding zone. Light tackle snobs chuckle derisively at the sight of a surf man wielding a nine foot spinning rod when casting worms or squid to school stripers off the beach. Yet if the fish are feeding in a slough 50 yards off the beach, there's not much the fisherman can do but use tackle capable of delivering his bait to that slough. Marine gamesters sometimes feed just outside the wash where a short cast will reach them. In those cases lighter tackle can be employed.

Casting live eels or whole squid or bunker requires heavy tackle. These baits must be lobbed out rather than cast, not only because of their bulk, but because a quick snap would tear out the hook.

As a general rule bait fishing tackle is heavier than the tackle used for artificial lures because of the weight of the terminal tackle. The rods with light tips just can't handle the heavy sinkers. A light, eight foot rod might be just fine for casting bucktail jigs to ten or twelve pound school stripers, but if you've got to cast three ounces of lead to hold bottom when fishing for two-pound kingfish you've got to go to heavier tackle.

Jetty fishing sometimes requires tackle that will overpower a fish. Fishing from a jetty for tautog with a light rod, for instance, is sheer folly. A tautog of average size, let's say four pounds, will dig for the rocks when hooked, hardly noticing that whippy rod bending ineffectually overhead. Tautog fishermen find stout tackle necessary even though their prey is not among the surf's heavyweights. Other fish that fall regularly to jetty jockeys might not be as obstinate as tautog, but they must be hauled up over the rocks. A long handled gaff helps, but a rod that will lift the fish up onto the jetty beats climbing down the rocks with a gaff in your hand. Fishermen who do that have uncertain futures. If you're tied into a 25 pound striper, however, you have no choice but to go down after him.

Sand spikes are among the surf fisherman's indispensable tools. It holds his spare rod, it holds his rod while he is baiting up and sometimes it holds his rod when he should be holding it.

The temptation when fishing is slow is to stock the rod in a sand spike, light a smoke, maybe pour a cup of coffee from a thermos and relax for a while. Any fish desirous of being caught will make its presence known by sending pulses up the line to the rod tip.

Fine, except that by the time the fisherman can grab the rod, the fish will have (1) taken the bait, (2) felt the hook, realized his mistake and fled, or, (3) sucked in the whole thing and hooked himself. The latter is least likely. Fish your rod. Have it in your hand when the strike comes.

All right, you haven't had a bite in 45 minutes, you need a smoke and a cup of coffee to buoy your lagging spirits. So set your rod in a sand spike. But in the name of Heaven make sure the spike is well anchored and the reel drag is loose enough to permit a fish to take line. If I had all the rods and reels ever pulled into the surf because some sloppy fisherman failed to sink his sand spike deep enough and left his drag socked up tight, I could open the biggest tackle store in the country.

THE SCIENCE OF BAIT FISHING

By combining a little deductive thinking with your powers of observation, bait fishing can be very rewarding. The selection of a bait should not be a haphazard process. While some of our marine gamefish are omnivorous, feeding on targets of opportunity, they can be highly selective at times. The fisherman who takes the time and effort to observe will be burdened with a heavy stringer.

There are predictable seasonal trends. Maine fishermen know early run stripers will be chasing herring. Cape Cod Canal fishermen watch for the midsummer run of squid. Jersey fishermen know that early fall will bring hordes of finger mullet into the surf and that predators will be gorging on them.

Seasons of plenty invite predators to glut themselves on specialties. I once watched a migration of sea worms drifting out of Great Salt Pond past the jetties that protect the Point Jude harbor. Literally millions of worms were floating, wriggling in the tide, and there were swirls where stripers took them. I saw the same thing in Coles River, a tidal river that enters the east side of Narragansett Bay. On those occasions the bass would hit nothing but worms.

In the mid 1960's there was a glut of mackerel along the south shore of New England. Casting from Narragansett's rocks one morn-

ing I foul hooked a mackerel on a bucktail jig, left it on and immediately hooked an eight pound bluefish, the only gamefish I saw
that day. Gamefish feed heavily on what is readily available during
these times of plenty.

These periods of plenty are so obvious that even the dullest of
fishermen cannot fail to observe and take advantage of them. But
there are more subtle, highly localized situations everywhere along
the coast. Only the careful student of the surf will recognize them
and profit. How, specifically, does one attain this degree of expertise
that will tell him what bait to use and when and how to use it? The
only answer is careful observation, experience, and common sense.
You must work at it, for it doesn't just come about.

Perhaps experience is the common denominator for expertise and
knowledge. You can't acquire it in a single season. Not until you have
fished the seasonal cycle many times, watching carefully and record-
ing in your mind if not in a fishing log just what happens from day to
day and week to week as the spring water warms to summer temperatures and then cools in the fall, do you gain experience. The
movements of fish are fairly predictable given the factors that
stimulate their movements. Fish respond to influences of tide, water
temperature, salinity, season, the mating urge, and many other
stimuli. Perhaps if you could obtain all the data and run it through a
computer you'd come up with a precise answer.

The best you can do is observe, record, and compare your observations over the years. Patterns will emerge. Whether you are a bait
fisherman or one totally committed to artificial lures, or as is more
often the case, something of both, you will be on your way to the
status of old pro. One of a small percentage of fishermen who catch
most of the fish.

You could concentrate on a small section of coast and learn it well.
Find out precisely what happens to every rock, every bar, every jetty,
every hole at every stage of the tide. Become an expert in that area
and you'll find before long that more of your casts are reaching fish.

Keep your eye on the person who consistently walks off the beach
carrying fish. In every area there are a few who score regularly, even
when others are going home to hamburger instead of fish dinners. If
a fisherman consistently catches fish while others are simply soaking
bait or feeding crabs you can be sure he's doing something right. You
can bet your new $90 spinning rod that it isn't just luck. Whatever he's
doing right is being done on purpose.

When I started fishing for shad a decade ago, I wasn't having any
luck at all. These big, scrappy herring make their spawning run up a
river not far from my home, and I was out evening after evening try-

ing to induce one to take one of my shad darts. There was one fellow who showed up every evening—a lean, spry old gent who invariably walked away carrying a few shad.

One Saturday morning I reported to the pool to find perhaps 15 fishermen circling it. One had two shad, another had one and the old fellow had six tied to a stringer and was fighting another. So what I did was sit on the bank for more than an hour just watching him fish. I noted where he cast his shad dart, how he retrieved, everything. Then I walked to the edge of the pool and in a half a dozen casts hooked my first shad.

I didn't land it. The blamed thing streaked the length of the pool ripping off line, then turned and headed back while I reeled desperately trying to spool the loose line. It jumped, threw the hook and was gone. But from then on I caught, or at least hooked shad on almost every trip.

The differences between what the successful fisherman does and what the flub-dub does may be small. Maybe he's threading his sea worm on the hook in a particular manner. Maybe he's casting to a tide rip near a submerged rock you don't even know is there. Maybe he left his squid out in the sun for a day to mature before using it. Watch him closely and then go and do thou likewise.

THE BAIT ITSELF

Hundreds of creatures that inhabit the sea provide fish with nourishment. Some fish such as tautog and kingfish have limited diets. Tautog browse the bottom rocks for bite-size creatures such as crabs and other crustaceans, mussels, clams and worms. Kingfish are also bottom browsers, limiting their intake to what can be picked up at that level. Fluke are mostly predators, feeding on small fish such as mummies (in New England they're mummies, in Jersey they're killies), silversides, small eels and such.

Bass and blues will at times eat just about anything including carrion. In that context, there's something I've come across in surf fishing I've often wondered about. I've never found a mummy (or killie) in the stomach of a striped bass, although these small baitfish are often present where the bass are feeding. A marine biologist who has examined the stomach contents of hundreds of stripers told me he had never found one in a striper's stomach either, but, out of scientific caution, would not flatly say stripers would not feed on these plentiful bait fish.

The most popular and probably the best all-around surf bait is the sea worm, a creature that appears on the diet of virtually every predator fish found in the surf. Only bluefish, which prefer their meals livelier, meatier, and generally in larger sizes, are not partial to sea worms. Even they will pick one up if it is handy.

There are two kinds of sea worms in common use, the clam worm and the blood worm. Both are present all along the coast, but most found in bait stores are dug in Maine where the great difference in the tide leaves large flats exposed.

Hook a seaworm this way for stripers, leaving a good part of the worm trailing. For tautog or kingfish cram the worm onto the hook, leaving little hanging.

Clam worms are more popular north of Long Island. From Long Island south the blood worms are more often used. This is probably because the blood worms are hardier and will stand up better during shipment. I watched fishermen using Maine blood worms as far south as the Roanoke River in North Carolina where spawning stripers were being caught.

For stripers, weaks, and fluke a whole worm is best. Just thread the head on the hook and let the rest of it stream out. Just cover the hook for tautog and kingfish. Otherwise you will be striking as the fish chew off the free end. On Cape Cod striper fishermen casting from the beach wad several worms on a large hook and score consistently.

Although usually fished on the bottom, often with a fishfinder rig, worms can also be fished under a bobber just as you once fished for sunfish with garden worms when you were a youngster. This method is effective from jetties, or the worm and bobber can be floated down an inlet tide. The worm should hang no more than a couple of feet below the bobber since bass and weaks will feed on or near the surface, or on or near the bottom—rarely in the middle zone.

Worms can also be used to sweeten bucktail jigs and metal lures, but they do not hold up well under the strain of casting. When bottom fishing with worms, use a float on the leader to hold the worm off the bottom and out of the reach of crabs. Crabs will quickly strip these soft-bodied creatures from the hook.

Crabs of various kinds are another favorite. In New Jersey, Delaware, and Maryland, crabs are considered fine bait for stripers. New England anglers spurn them as striper bait.

That crabs will catch stripers in New England was brought home to me one fall on a day when Andy Cameron, a neighbor, and I spent two hours flogging the surf around Point Judith with plugs. Disgusted, finally, we gave up and headed for home. Seeing some fishermen on Narragansett's rocks we stopped, only to find they were tautog fishermen. Andy, who sniffs imperiously at any fish that does not take an artificial lure, turned to go when I spotted two stripers, one of about a dozen pounds and the other perhaps two pounds lighter, lying in a cleft in the rocks.

"Who caught them?" I asked a youngster.

The youngster pointed to a man sitting on the rock holding a rod. He was bottom fishing.

"No," the fisherman told me, "I wan't fishing for bass. I'm after tautog. But a while ago something started off with my bait and it turned out to be a striper. Then I got another one right after that. I'm using crabs. Never knew stripers hit crabs." Well, I knew it, but being a Yankee and not a Jersey fisherman, I'd never tried them.

There is no better bait for tautog than fiddler crabs, but these small crustaceans are getting scarce, at least in my part of the country. Time was when I could walk the sod bank of a tidal river and fill a bucket in short order. Now I'm hard put to get enough for a fishing trip. Fiddlers are hooked by breaking off the large claw and inserting the hook through the hole.

Other crabs, and there are several varieties used, are either quartered or fished whole depending on the size. Quartered, they leak blood and body juices to form a tasty chum line. Shedder crabs (those about to shed their shells) and soft shelled crabs (those which have shed their outer covering and are in the process of growing new ones) are preferred by many striper fishermen. The soft shelled crabs must be tied to the hook since they are too soft to be held by the barb.

Skimmer clams, also called surf clams, hard-shelled clams, also known as quahogs, razor clams, soft shelled clams, or steamers, are all used for bait. Skimmer clams are often used as bait for stripers from Long Island south, but Yankee surfers haven't yet learned that these huge bivalves make prime bass bait. Several years ago literally millions of small skimmers were washed up on the beach at Newport, R.I. Many died to be washed back to sea on the outgoing tide. I learned later that a few local fishermen, fishing the beach at night after the crowds had gone, and using these clams for bait, racked up impressive catches of striped bass.

You can harvest your own skimmer clams (but check with your local laws first) by wading barefooted at low tide. You'll feel the clams partly buried in the sand with your feet.

Once while gathering skimmers on Cape Cod I made a grand discovery. I was opening the clams and storing the meat in plastic bags to freeze for later use as bait for cod and winter flounder. In the process it occurred to me that the large muscles holding the shells together might be good to eat. I fried some in butter and found them to be almost identical to scallops in taste. I haven't thrown away a skimmer clam muscle or used one for bait since.

The soft parts of clams won't hold on the hook, so I use them as chum, tossing them into the water. Those that the gulls don't get first sink slowly and send off appealing scents that allure gamefish. A substantial gob of clam meat on a 3/0 hook is considered about right for stripers. Smaller pieces are used for tautog. Kingfish prefer bite-size chunks, and winter flounder require only enough to cover the point of the hook.

Early run tautog fishermen in Rhode Island use whole mussels for bait, opening the shell and inserting the hook into the tough part of the meat. Shell and all are cast, but gently, because there is not much substance to a mussel which can fall off the hook easily.

A good way to fish soft shell clams for tautog is to hook them through the neck and then crush the shell before casting. Tautog don't mind the shells at all. They have the equipment to handle them.

Eels are universally regarded as perhaps the most consistently effective bait for stripers and blues, although many hesitate to use them when bluefish are present. I've reeled in a half an eel more than once when these sea-going butchers were on the prowl.

Eels are fished live by hooking them through the jaw and letting them swim freely. At inlets and river mouths the fishermen let the bait drift out with the tide on an open bail or with the reel in free spool. When a fish takes it he's allowed to run. Some wait until the first run stops and the fish sets off again before trying to set the hook. The theory is that the fish runs, then pauses to ingest his meal before moving on. Sometimes this has worked for me, but other times it hasn't. Maybe the difference is in the individual fish.

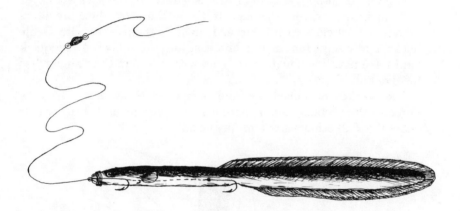

Dead eels are strung on wire or plumber's chain with a hook protruding from the vent and another hook sometimes arming the head. They are retrieved slowly along the bottom, usually at night, although they will catch fish in the daytime as well. Eels cast miserably, by the way.

There is one school that insists strung eels are best when over-ripe. Some go to the extreme of aging the cadavers. Those who do this are often asked to fish alone. Aged eels are not good company, even on a wind-swept jetty.

Eel skins are also used effectively on eel bobs or eel rigs. The skin is turned inside-out, thus presenting a more visible translucent bluish color, and tied to the rig. The rig itself is no more than a lead head with a ring to which the skin is attached. Tandem hooks snelled on wire complete the rig. An opening in the head permits water to flow through the skin during the retrieve, giving the whole rig a life-like appearance. For years this was the favorite lure for both stripers and blues along the Cape Cod Canal.

If you're going to handle eels, by the way, be prepared to get thoroughly mucked up by their slime. Wetting your hands and then coating them with sand helps in gripping these slimy critters. Or they can be handled with a coarse, dry rag.

The mossbunker, called *menhaden* (its Indian name in New England), or pogy (not to be confused with porgy, another name for scup), is a favorite of both bass and blues. It is an oily fish, a member of the herring family. For the past few years they have been at the top of a population cycle and are prolific.

Only rarely is a surf fisherman able to fish live bunker. Boat fishermen capture them and keep them alive in aerated bait wells, but there is no easy way a pogy tank can be carried on the beach, even in a beach buggy. Bunker are fished live in the surf whenever fishermen are fortunate enough to be on the spot when predators drive a school close to the shore. They arm themselves with treble hooks, add weight for casting, and cast into the school. A few quick yanks are usually enough to connect with flesh, and the angler has his live bait.

The bunker is lobbed out and permitted to swim freely. Live bunker have probably taken more big bass over the past three or four years than all other baits and lures combined.

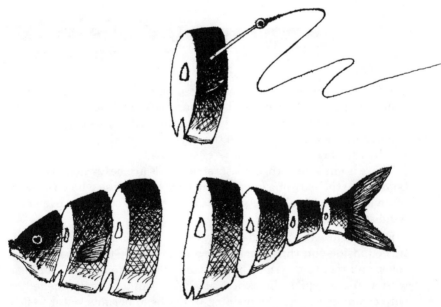

To fish cut bait such as bunker, herring, mackerel or butterfish, slice and hook as shown.

A dead bunker is chunked, threaded on a hook, and fished on the bottom. It will attract stripers, blues, weaks, and sometimes fluke.

Herring, more properly called alewives, are fished the same way. Again the problem of keeping them alive makes fishing them live from the beach or jetty impractical. Only in the spring when they swarm into the river to spawn are they available to fishermen. They can be snatched or netted at river mouths and inlets and live-lined. For cut bait I simply halve a herring by cutting on a diagonal line from just behind the head to the vent. The head half seems to be best.

Silversides, sand eels, spearing, all are excellent surf baits when used either whole or cut. These silvery fish are appealing to blues, weaks, and stripers, and are particularly effective for fluke. For larger fish, bass and blues, jam several on a hook; for weaks, one or two will do the trick. Hang a single fish on a bucktail jig for best results with fluke.

South of Long Island the mullet is a favorite. Another oily fish, it leaves the bays and backwaters and appears in the surf in the early fall. They stay alive in a bait bucket, but most fish them whole or chunked. These are finger mullet, averaging three to four inches in length.

New Englanders find mackerel is an excellent bait for stripers and blues. These pelagic fish are rarely found in the warmer waters south of Cape Cod in the summer. Because they cannot easily be kept alive they are rarely fished alive from the beach, but boat fishermen live-line them for bass and blues with excellent results. Yankee surfmen often bait with chunks of cut mackerel from the beach. Maryland, Delaware, New Jersey, and Long Island anglers can stock up when the spring migration of mackerel passes off shore in late April or early May.

Squid is a universal bait that takes most gamefish. Large stripers take whole or large chunks of squid. When cut, the head is usually used. Smaller pieces take blues, kings and weaks. Strip baits cut from squid are effective for most gamefish and a strip added to a bucktail jig or metal lure gives the lure irresistible appeal.

Other fish are also good bait. A fine fall bait for bluefish is chunks cut from a snapper blue, one of the six to eight inch youngsters that abound in harbors and off jetties in the early fall. The first bluefish you catch can be chunked and used to catch more. A strip of belly cut from a fluke is a favorite bait for fluke or you can cut the strip from a sea robin or other trash fish. Delaware, Maryland, and South Jersey fishermen cut a small, oily fish called the Norfolk spot while butterfish are popular all along the coast.

An inch long crustacean, the sand bug, found burrowed into the sand at the water's edge can be threaded on a hook for stripers or tautog. Some rate them above crabs for tautog.

Grass shrimp, which abound in tidal rivers, bays, and backwaters are favorites of weakfish and stripers. However these small (half inch) creatures are fragile and a thin wire hook must be used.

FRESH BAIT

Keeping your bait fresh is a key to successful bait fishing. Some species can be kept alive. Eels, for instance, will live for hours in wet sea weed. In fact you may have trouble killing an eel. The damned things have a tenacity that is unbelievable. I have kept eels all summer in a wire cage hung under a dock. Mummies, too, can be kept alive for a considerable time in wet seaweed. Finger mullet will live in a well-aerated bait bucket for the duration of a day's fishing. Sea worms remain feisty if kept cool and damp in seaweed. They can be kept for considerable periods in the family refrigerator provided they are stirred up a little every day so they don't ball up. Crabs will remain happy and lively if a piece of wet burlap is thrown over them and they are kept cool. Grass shrimp need mostly to be kept cool and moist.

Most salt water baitfish such as mackerel, bunker, and herring turn belly up within minutes in an ordinary bait bucket. Squid, as far as I know, can't be kept alive at all. They must be frozen if they are to be kept for any length of time.

Boat fishermen have an advantage here. Bait wells or tanks with circulating water will keep bunker, herring or mackerel alive for indefinite periods. Surf fishermen can't carry circulating tanks. However in South Jersey, Delaware and Maryland, those with beach buggies mount coolers on them, install aerators, and carry spot or mullet for live bait fishing from the beach. The larger bait fish would not survive very long.

Clams can be kept alive under refrigeration for days. Once dead they are best used immediately or frozen.

Keeping bait cool is usually the best way to keep it fresh. Ice, of course, is the best cooling agent, but damp seaweed will save bait for a surprisingly long time. One word of warning. Never wet sea worms with fresh water. Nothing kills them quicker, and dead sea worms will deteriorate almost before your eyes.

You can find a lot of bait by yourself, but check the local laws. Clams and quahogs are available in most bays and tidal rivers, and sea worms live alongside the clams. Mummies readily enter minnow traps baited with a few crushed mussels or clams. Mussels can be picked off the rocks at low tide. Eels can be caught with hook and line in any tidal river, or they can be taken in eel pots or even ordinary eel traps baited with fish heads. Mullet are easily netted when they appear in the surf in September. Green crabs infest any rocky shoreline. Just put a ripe fish head in any tidal pool and stand by to reap the harvest. River herring swarm in tidal rivers every spring. You can snatch them with treble hooks, catch them in dip nets, or do as I do, catch them on ultra-light fresh water tackle using a tiny shad dart as a lure. They can be frozen or salted down. Yankee fishermen can go a hundred yards off shore in many places and jig up enough mackerel for a season of fishing in a few hours. Further south fishermen must stock up during the spring and fall migrations. They can be salted down or frozen for later use. A hand seine worked along the edge of a set of eel grass will net a supply of grass shrimp in short order.

A season's supply of squid can often be jigged up in a few hours from a pier or bridge by Yankee fishermen. At the Goat Island Causeway in Newport harbor, for instance, dozens of squid jiggers can be found on any June evening. They use brightly-colored plastic jigs armed with dozens of sharp, upturned points. When the squid attack the jigs, their tentacles become tangled in the points. They are then reeled in and shaken off into a bucket. Squid isn't only for bait. Take some, clean and peel them, cut them into strips, roll in a batter and deep fry for two minutes. Absolutely delicious.

Very often you can catch your bait right where you're fishing. One day last summer when the fluke off the Point Jude breakwater were uncooperative, we took a dead sea robin someone had left on the rocks, tied a weight to it, and tossed it in the water. After a few minutes it could be drawn out slowly and the crabs shaken off in a bucket. We then moved to the end of the breakwater where we were rewarded with a baker's dozen of tautog.

I have often turned over stones along the beach for crabs and sea worms, and even the ever-present periwinkles can be used for bait. Crush them, line them up on a hook, and they will take tautog.

There is much more bait available along the Atlantic Coast. Just about any of the hundreds of creatures that share the environment of predator fish is potential bait. But remember that taste often varies according to season or abundance of forage. Study the surf scene, know what's going on before you bait up. Make sure your bait is in a condition to attract the gamefish you're trying to interest. Present it properly, and get ready to set the hook.

Section 4

Fish of the North Atlantic Coast

Now it's time to meet the quarry and sort it out by its regional name. Regional names can be confusing. Many years ago I decided to try some surf fishing during a family camping trip to Arcadia National Park in Maine. The park ranger told me some nice sea perch might be caught along the rocky shore. Sea perch, as it turned out, were those pesky little bait stealers that Southern New Englanders call choggies and others call bergalls or cunners. Let's start with striped bass.

The striper is the aristocrat of surf fish. It has dignity, grace, strength, beauty—all the attributes of nobility. Known as striper or striped bass over much of its range; south of Delaware Bay it is the rock or rock fish.

There are bluefish—brawling, tough, possibly the nastiest of all creatures in a world in which competition for survival transcends all other considerations. The prince of gluttony; it feeds upon virtually anything that will either fit whole in its mouth or can be torn by those savage teeth. That includes any portion of a fisherman's anatomy that can be reached.

Fluke, bottom-hugging doormats whose swiftness in the pursuit of their prey belies their awkward shape. Neither a determined fighter nor a fish of beauty, its willingness to cooperate has saved the day for many a surf fisherman. Call it a fluke if you're from Massachusetts, a summer flounder in Rhode Island, a fluke in New York or New Jersey, and a flounder south of Delaware Bay.

Weakfish, squeteague in New England, and trout from Delaware south, is a lusty, colorful, free-swimming beauty, designed by someone who was bent on creating the perfect fish for light tackle salt water angling.

Tautog, blackfish in parts of New York and New Jersey, and just plain "tog" farther south are dark-visaged, broad-shouldered brutes that prowl the rocky bottom feeding on crabs, clams, worms and, terminal tackle.

These are the most sought-after surf species, but not the only ones caught by any means. In New England pollock, racy relatives of the cod, move close to shore in early winter to extend the surf fishing season for those who hate to quit. Cod, these deep water plug uglies, normally caught miles from shore, move in on New England beaches during the winter where they are caught by frost-proof Yankees fishing with salt water ice in their guides, hand warmers in their pockets, and flagons of 80 proof defroster close by. Winter flounder, smaller cousins of fluke, cold water fish who spend their summers in the deep, return to bays and backwaters in the winter and are caught in spring and fall in passage to and from their winter homes.

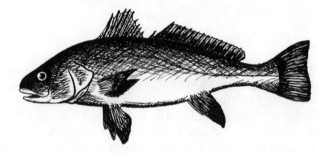

Channel Bass

Bonito, swift members of the tuna family, flash into the beach on occasion to raid the bait schools. Channel bass, which formerly were regular visitors to the South Jersey beaches, rarely occur north of Assateague Island these days. Scup, silvery ocean panfish, live over sandy bottoms and are taken from jetties. Black drum, huge, blocky relatives of the channel bass are caught mostly as they spawn in Delaware Bay and other inland waters, but only occasionally by surf fishermen. Then there are those fish we don't want to catch but often do. Such are as sea robins, gaudy and greedy bottom dwellers, persistent in their designs on baited hooks. Cunner, also known as choggies and bergalls, sharp-toothed bait stealers that swarm around jetties and off rocky shores. Dogfish, also called sand sharks, cause Cape Cod surf fishermen to reel in their baits and go off cursing. Skate, whip-tailed uglies with spreading wings, determined attackers of any kind of bait an angler casts. You will also find blowfish, more sharp-toothed bait stealers whose depradations angered Long Island and New Jersey fishermen until they discovered the little rascals carry some small, but tasty fillets.

With that brief introduction out of the way let's look more closely into the lives and habits of these fish.

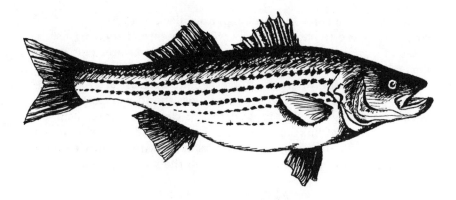

STRIPED BASS (ROCK)

Ask a surf fisherman what fish he'd most like to catch. Chances are he'll say striped bass. If you don't understand why, you're missing the whole point of surf fishing.

Striped bass embody the spirit, the mystique of the surf. They are more of the surf than any other creature. No other fish takes such liberties, or uses that dynamic, untameable element so effectively. The striper's appearance reflects the life it leads — sleek lines with a muscular body and a broad tail designed to power through the turbulent water. It's the perfect physique for a creature that spends so much of its life in that riotous place where the ocean collides with the shore.

Not all of its life by any means. Striped bass or Rock are born in slow-moving freshwater rivers and spend the first two or three years of life in quiet estuary waters. When they migrate northward along the coast, smaller fish seek out tidal rivers where they feed on shrimp and small baitfish. Larger bass enter such places as Narragansett Bay or Pleasant Bay on Cape Cod to chase the spring run of alewives and often linger there to feed on menhaden. Some inland states have taken advantage of their ability to thrive in fresh water and have started extensive stocking programs in lakes. Most are successful.

Striped bass are caught in many ways and in many places, but our concern in this book is for those in the surf. If you're interested in reading more about this great Atlantic fish, try John Cole's *STRIP-ER: A Story of Fish and Man* (Little, Brown & Co. - 1978).

This is the only large marine game fish that consistently appears within casting distance of the shore. This alone is enough to endear them to surf casters — even without their other attributes, gameness, a willingness to take a bait or lure, their quality as table fare. They present a challenge. Stripers are not pushovers by any means. To catch them consistently one must be aware of their habits, their dietary preferences, their seasonal and daily movements as influenced by water temperature, tides, currents and the movement of bait. Many factors are involved; not all of them easily perceived or understood.

Their dietary preferences vary according to the place, the season and the type of bait present. They can be highly selective feeders, ignoring all baits and lures except for the specific bait, or representation thereof, they happen to be feeding on at the moment. Or they might be feeding on targets of opportunity, willing to sample anything that comes along.

Selective feeding occurs when schooled bait is present. It can be herring, menhaden, mackerel, sand eels, squid, or even shrimp. Hunting is easy then. Bass gather around the bait schools and feed by picking off stragglers or herding the bait before slashing through it. Anglers using lures resembling the bait, or the bait itself, will score.

As a general rule the smaller fish are more active and aggressive than larger ones and are more likely to take artificial lures. Most big fish (those of 30 pounds or more) are taken by anglers using bait. Most older bass are unwilling to use the energy to chase a lure when they can laze along the bottom and pick up a dead squid or a chunk of bunker.

As noble as they are, striped bass are not above scavenging. There's a theory that aggressiveness in striped bass is genetic and that quality of aggressiveness is declining as more aggressive fish are caught. These fish are more susceptible to artificial lures, the theory goes. As these fish fall prey to their rambunctiousness, the characteristic is lost to the gene pool, leaving the more timid individuals to perpetuate the species.

Could be. It's an interesting theory, and it could explain why bait fishing seems to be more productive than it once was.

Regardless of that theory, the fact is that there are fewer striped bass as we move into the 1980's. The future of the species is uncertain at best. That the species has been in a decline along the Atlantic Coast for a decade can be documented in commercial catch records (there are no reliable sport catch records) and in the results of young-of-the-year surveys taken annually in Chesapeake Bay, the source of most of the coastal striper stocks.

The commercial catch records show that even under increasing fishing activity brought about by high market demand, the catch has fallen off year by year, while alarming statistics compiled by biologists who survey the spawning grounds show that fewer fish are being produced each year. Optimists hope a natural cycle will ultimately replenish the dwindling stocks; alarmists predict extinction of the species unless conservation measures are taken.

Most coastal states are considering conservation measures. They include larger length limits, daily bag limits, restrictions on commercial netters, bans on the sale of stripers, high license fee for commercial fishermen — all aimed at reducing catch mortality. Whether they will help remains to be seen.

Why are the stocks declining? Theories abound; hard evidence is hard to come by. Studies show larval bass taken from the Hudson River, Delaware Bay, Chesapeake Bay and Albemarle Sound contain heavy metals and chemical pollutants that weaken the tiny fish and imperil survival. Other studies show the survival of larval stripers, aside from any pollution problems, is largely dependent on the presence of nutrients in the water at that critical time when they have absorbed their yolk sacs and are ready to begin feeding.

Striped bass abundance depends on a recurring phenomenon known as the dominant year hatch. Because of this, dramatic peaks and valleys of abundance have occurred over the years. A series of poor spawning years, the intervals varying, reduce the stocks. Then will come a dominant year hatch and great numbers of small fish will enter the fishery. Biologists tell us that relatively few adult fish are needed to produce a dominant year hatch, indicating that the cause is environmental. That is, in a given year environmental factors such as water temperature, salinity, the presence of nutrients and so forth permit greater numbers of young to survive. But man's impact on the environment could have interrupted this natural process. The fish now must contend with the still unmeasured effect of man's misuse of the environment.

Other marine game fish are less vulnerable. They spawn and spend much of their lives in the open sea, still relatively free from pollution. Striped bass are anadromous fish, they spawn in fresh water rivers that drain farmlands (pesticides and herbicides), urban areas (municipal sewage) and industrial areas (all manner of heavy metals and toxic chemicals. They spend their early years in bays and river systems where conditions are no better, and even when they migrate to ocean waters they stay close to shore in those waters most affected by pollution.

So striped bass, our most prized marine game fish, may well be at the questionable mercy of civilization that historically has placed the survival of wild creatures below other priorities.

The situation is not hopeless. Government concern joins the concern of sport fishermen. Federally financed studies into the reasons for the decline are under way. Other studies are aimed at determining as precisely as possible how many fish are left. Support for these studies comes from both commercial and recreational fishermen who are beginning to realize that striped bass can be an exhaustible resource.

So long as we still have striped bass, let's take a look at the seasonal movements of this royal fish of the surf.

The northward migration of Chesapeake Bay fish begins in early April. Fishermen in Maryland and Delaware report their first, scattered catches about the first of April and activity increases daily until the bulk of the migration moves past in May. These areas do not have large resident populations during the summer months. Fishing is fair in the spring, dies off until early October, and then spurts until the fish have again passed in late November. Fall fishing is by far the best.

The season begins about a week later in New Jersey. Long Island gets the vanguard in late April as does the south shore of Rhode Island. I have caught stripers in the surf in Rhode Island as early as April 15, but it is well after that before the main body of the migration arrives.

Fish that breed in the Hudson move out into the salt water in May and spread through the waters at the western end of Long Island and down the North Jersey coast where they remain all summer.

In Massachusetts school fish appear in the surf at Popponesset Beach on Cape Cod and off Gooseberry Island on the south shore late in May. Larger fish appear about that same time to chase herring in the Cape Cod Canal. In early June they are found off Plum Island on the Massachusetts north shore, and a week or so later are spreading all along the Maine Coast.

New England has good striper fishing all summer, as does Long Island and North Jersey, but during the warm weather the best fishing is found at night.

Tagging returns have pretty well established that most of New England's fish come from the Chesapeake Bay area. Hudson River fish apparently do not move much farther than Long Island and North Jersey. There are breeding populations of stripers in the St. Lawrence and St. John's Rivers in Canada, but whether these fish make up any portion of Maine's summer population I don't know.

Some northern rivers have wintering over-populations of striped bass, but they are not active in the cold weather and seldom if ever run out to sea. The Thames River in New London, Conn., Narrow River in Narragansett, R.I., and the Taunton River in Massachusetts all hold winter populations and produce fish during the winter for those hardy enough to fish for them. I caught a 14 pounder from the warm water discharge of the Brayton Point power plant in Swansea, Mass., in February four years ago. According to the Maine Department of Sea and Shore Fisheries, there was a winter commercial fishery for stripers in the Kennebec River at the turn of the century.

Why there is no breeding population in New England is difficult to understand in view of the fact that stripers spawn in rivers both to the north and south. It is thought by some that stripers may have bred in the Connecticut River at one time. If so, dams probably halted the upstream runs and the strain gradually died out, just as the Atlantic salmon that spawned in the Connecticut River system has died out. Efforts are now being made to restore the salmon population, but nothing is being done about restoring stripers. The Thames, Taunton, and Merrimac Rivers may all have hosted breeding populations at one time.

It is unlikely that a breeding population will regenerate by itself. A study conducted some years ago by the University of Rhode Island showed that approximately 95 per cent of the stripers in local waters were males — a sexual balance that would hardly encourage reproduction.

While some stripers elect to stay in New England's frigid waters all winter, most migrate back to the more amenable climate of the middle south for the winter. Early September sees them gathering to leave Maine. Massachusetts stripers are on the move by October 1, although good fishing continues for most of the month. I have had good fishing days late in October in Massachusetts and there was one memorable November day at Gooseberry Island when almost every cast brought a strike.

Long Island and New Jersey anglers enjoy good surf fishing for striped bass well into November, and South Jersey, Delaware, and Maryland fishermen are still taking stripers from beaches and jetties in early December. The season ends officially on December 31 in New Jersey.

Early season stripers are sluggish and are more easily taken on bait. With the water still retaining some of winter's chill and the metabolism still a good way from peak form, these first-of-the-season stripers seem to prefer picking up a bottom bait to chasing a plug. As the water warms they become more active and lure fishermen begin scoring. This is true all along the coast, whether in April at Indian River Inlet, May at Sandy Hook, or June at Popponesset Beach. Worms are the best early spring baits. Herring and bunker take big fish since these are major items on the diet this time of year. Bunker continues as a favorite bait well into the summer wherever they are present. Eels and squid are prime warm water baits.

But when the bass school up for the fall migration, hardware takes over. Along the coast top water lures excite these rambunctious and always hungry migrating fish which are feeding heavily on bunker, sand eels, butterfish and mackerel. Lure pattern or color doesn't seem to make much difference at this point. These fish are fattening up for the long trip south. If it moves, they'll attack it.

Here are some tips to catch more stripers. First, members of Stripers Unlimited kept records of their catches one year and the results showed that stripers get virtually all their food either on the bottom or in the top layer of water. Thus if you are casting in say, 15 feet of water and retrieving your lure at the seven foot depth you're probably dragging it through barren water. Fish either top or bottom, not in between.

Stripers are most active when the water temperature is between 55 and 65 degrees. Colder or warmer than that and their metabolism slows. This is the optimum temperature when they are the most active and when they are most likely to take a lure or bait.

Old timers say, and my experience bears this out, that striper fishing is best following a full moon, or the downside of the moon as they say. The higher tides during the period of the full moon stir up more action in the water and trigger the feeding urge. Whatever the reason, you'll be adding to your chances if you schedule your striper trips for the period immediately following a full moon.

Stripers seem to be happiest in the rough water. Veteran surf men curse the off-shore breeze that flattens the surf. They want to see white water breaking along the beach and over the ends of the breakwaters and jetties. This isn't simply because bass like to test their strength in a hostile environment, bait is tumbled about in the rough water and stripers find dining easier on the disoriented baitfish.

For the past year or so those who prefer stripers over blues have often been faced with the option of casting to schools of feeding bluefish or catching nothing at all. When a school of blues breaks close to the beach, it seems that's all for stripers. But that's not necessarily so. The next time this happens put on a bucktail jig with a strip of pork rind and fish it along the bottom underneath the blues or in back of them. Stripers, less aggressive than bluefish, sometimes lie under these rampaging schools of choppers and feed quietly on the chunks of fish that drift down in their wake. If you can sink your jig through the blues, which often isn't easy because the blues are ready to hit anything moving in the water, you can pick up striped bass.

Here's another tip. Big stripers sometimes feed heavily on sand eels, small, elongated silvery baitfish, and ignore the full-sized swimming and popping plugs being thrown at them. You can imagine how this peeves surf casters who know the fish are there, but can't draw a strike. If sand eels are present, try tying on a simple, white bucktail as a dropper and see what happens.

The above isn't all you'll want to know about stripers and striper fishing by any means, but it's a starting point. Whether we'll even have striped bass around in the next few years isn't certain in view of the breeding failures of the last few years. There's one way you can help a little. When you've caught enough for your needs, release the rest. And boycott those tournaments that put a premium on striped bass cadavers.

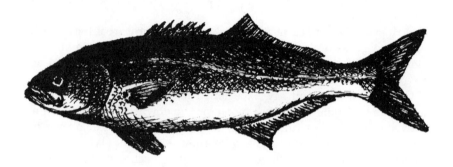

BLUEFISH

There are purists among surf fishermen, just as there are among fresh water fly fishermen. A striped bass addict who I know will have nothing at all to do with bluefish. He calls them "Piranhas" and leaves the beach in a sulk when the blues move in. This fisherman's the loser for this attitude. As the coastal population of striped bass has declined, the stocks of bluefish has increased. Surf fishermen all along the coast have been joyfully taking advantage of this proliferation of riches.

Bluefish first appear in Maryland and Delaware in late April or early May. I have caught them in Chesapeake Bay in mid-April. They are less tolerant of cold water than striped bass, preferring a range of 65 to 85 degrees, but they will move into 60 degree water. Mid-May finds them off New Jersey, a week later they are at Montauk and from there they quickly invade southern New England.

Like many salt water fish, bluefish are cyclical with populations rising and falling in an irregular pattern over the years. In the late 1940's and early 50's bluefish were a rarity over their entire range; then in the mid-fifties they began to trickle in. By the mid-sixties we had a good thing going. The explosion came in the early 1970's. They swarmed in such numbers that we tired of catching them on standard surf tackle and went to fly rodding. I took blues up to 12 pounds on my sea-going fly rod.

Of all the characteristics possessed by bluefish, gluttony is the most

prominent. When they are in a feeding frenzy they will attack anything that moves. Lure color, shape or size is not important then;
movement is all that counts. When rampaging blues move in close to
bathing beaches, life guards whistle bathers to shore. Sections of
Cape Cod beaches have to be closed from time to time because of
bluefish. There are documented cases of bathers being attacked.

Until the early 70's Cape Cod stood as a northern barrier to bluefish
migrations. The colder water inside Cape Cod Bay, influenced by
Arctic currents that flow into the Gulf of Maine, discouraged the fish
from moving north of the Cape. But that's no longer true. Huge
schools spend the summer in Cape Cod Bay, infesting the waters off
Boston's North Shore and even filtering into Maine. Those visits to
Maine are sporadic and unpredictable. They may appear briefly and
then move out, or they may stay for weeks. Some years they don't
show at all.

Why they are suddenly infesting those colder waters is not clear. A
proliferation of bunker in those waters may be the answer, or it may
simply be a case of over-crowding. The fish may instinctively deploy
when there are too many of them for the available food supply in their
regular hunting grounds.

Blues are strong and durable fighters. Experienced surf men can
tell almost instantly whether they have hooked a bluefish or a striper
by the power and speed of the battler. When I hooked my first
bluefish in the surf many years ago I was sure I had a big bass. The
fish hit a yellow Gibbs Darter in the surf off Point Jude and as the
battle wore on I became more convinced that I at last had a striper of
20 pounds or more. It turned out to be an eight pound bluefish.

Not only are they stronger than bass, but blues will jump unlike
stripers. I've had as many as half a dozen jumps from a single
bluefish. And where a striper will give up once he's in the wash, a blue
continues the battle right up onto the dry sand. The angler who
values his skin carries a club, also known as a priest, when blue-
fishing. Applied vigorously between the eyes, this takes the
starch out of a beached blue and permits the angler to extract the
hook with some assurance his own flesh will not be shredded. Jaws
and teeth that can easily chop an eel or a herring in half can do a
fearful job on a finger. I have twice rushed careless fishermen to hos-
pitals, their hands so badly mangled that more was needed than the
first aid that could be administered on the beach. One of them gave
his bluefish away. Said he wouldn't feel right eating a fish that had
tried to eat him first.

It's because of this that many bluefish are wasted. A fish that has
been beaten insensible cannot be returned to the water to fight again
another day, and in times of plenty fishermen sometimes find them-

selves with more bluefish than they can possibly use. The surplus too often end up in the garbage, a shameful end to these tenacious and spirited gamefish.

Since the diets of bluefish and stripers are similar, the continued abundance of bluefish and their obvious success in breeding probably needs some explanation, but I don't have it. Bluefish, too, have been found with high levels of DDT. Perhaps because they are rather oily fish, the chemical does not concentrate in the reproductive assembly. The fact that they spawn in the open sea rather than in the more polluted rivers may have something to do with it.

As gluttonous as they are (blues will sometimes feed until gorged, regurgitate, and then resume feeding) they can be highly selective feeders. Large schools of bait, mackerel, squid, butterfish, mullet, and bunker seem to trigger this gluttony, but when the bait schools are not present they are more likely to cruise the bottom looking for eels. There are periods every season when live eels seem to be the only bait that will bring response, and at other times only cut mackerel will satisfy their appetites.

Nor will they hesitate to feed on the flesh of their bretheren. One of the most popular baits for blues all along the coast last year was chunked or sliced snapper blue. I was fishing the Delaware beach just north of Indian River Inlet a few autumns ago with plugs and was having no luck at all. Then I fell into conversation with a fisherman who had half a dozen blues on the beach, all caught on chunks cut from a bluefish he had caught the day before. I sliced a piece of the dead bluefish, hung it on a bucktail jig and was immediately rewarded.

Unlike stripers, which spend much of their lives within a cast of the beach, blues are wide-ranging—sometimes appearing well out to sea and sometimes pushing bait right up into the wash. Their visits to shore are not always predictable. Boat fishermen can often find them in the same spot all season, year after year, but surf fishermen must rely on local conditions to draw them in. I recall a week on Nausett Beach a dozen years ago when blues appeared at a certain bar an hour before high tide every day. Beach buggies were parked bumper to bumper and fishermen elbowed for casting space at the appointed hour every day.

But more often fishing for blues from the beach is a hit and run affair. Swiftly-moving schools close in on pods of bait, tear through them and then go down to appear minutes later hundreds of yards away. Often a fisherman has time to haul but a single fish from the school before it moves on. Fishermen exhaust themselves slogging through beach sand in waders trying to keep up with moving schools.

Bait fishermen doze for long periods while their rods stand in sand spikes, their lines angling straight and still out into the water and then spend frantic minutes battling fish, re-baiting and casting until the blues scatter to find other feeding grounds.

A high surf does not discourage them, although silted water and water filled with weed keeps them away. Where stripers seem to lie low and feed little when the surf is flat and the sun is high, blues have no such hang-ups. They will appear almost any time, anywhere, as long as there is bait. You can often see a school surface close to shore on a day when the sea is teacup calm.

Some have written that blues are not nighttime feeders, but I can testify otherwise. Time and again I've caught bluefish at night on eels, eel rigs, and artificial lures. The dawn often finds surf anglers heading for home with mixed strings of bass, blues, and weakfish. Eels, which are surely among the favorites of hungry bluefish, move about more freely at night and blues actively hunt them down.

It is when they are stoking up for the southward migration that they are most susceptible to artificial lures. In the cooling waters with the urge to migrate rising in them, blues feed heavily and will slash at any lure that swims across their vision.

Their stay in northern waters is shorter than it is for stripers. Northern New England sees the last of them in September. Southern New England anglers have them until early October, with a mid-month northeast storm often putting an end to their stay. Long Island and North Jersey fishermen enjoy their presence until late in the month, and South Jersey, Delaware, and Maryland fishermen see their best fishing in late October and well into November.

WEAKFISH

Weakfish appear to be in abundance after a long period of scarcity. In the late 1940's Southern New Englanders had squeteage, to give them their Yankee name, without end. They were mostly small fish, averaging a couple of pounds, with a few larger ones (called tide runners) mixed in to add spice. Then they disappeared without a trace.

This was not a gradual disappearance. They were there one year and gone the next as if stricken by a plague. At the same time fishermen to the south saw a marked decrease in the numbers of weakfish in their waters. Long Island and Jersey fishermen found a few, but for all practical pruposes the weakfish fishery was dead.

This situation remained for almost 20 years. Why the weakfish disappeared has been the subject of much debate. Some feel it was the resurgence of the bluefish that kept them away, but that doesn't hold

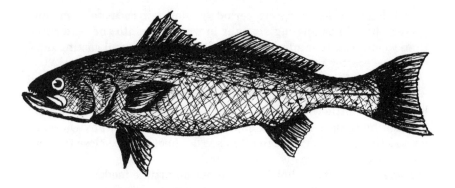

up in light of the present big cycle of both fish which are living together all along the coast. Not in perfect harmony, though! I have twice in the past two years seen weakfish come ashore with substantial amounts of flesh missing, bitten off as they struggled against the rod.

Others feel the disappearance of the grass shrimp in inland waters may have had something to do with their demise since these tiny shrimp are the mainstay of the diets of young weaks. Others guess it was just a natural cycle.

Whatever the reason, they were not with us for many years. Then in the fall of 1969 while fishing in Narragansett Bay for winter flounder, I caught four small young weakfish. I saw none in 1970, although I heard of a few being caught. Then in 1971 they suddenly reappeared in their old haunts. There was one main difference. Where in the late 1940's most were small fish, now the average size was perhaps four pounds, with many running to eight and ten. Some ran to 12 pounds, a size almost unheard of in the old days. They have been coming back regularly since then. All along the shore from Ocean City, Maryland to Massachusetts there are more and bigger weakfish.

Weakfish arrive off the Maryland-Delaware shore in early May and work way rapidly up the coast. New England's south shore usually gets them before the end of May. They occur only rarely in the colder waters north of Cape Cod. Weakfish are most active in water temperatures over 65 degrees.

Few Yankee surf men seek them in the surf. In their northern range weaks are bay fish and are not commonly found along the ocean front. But from Long Island south, surf and jetty anglers find them a prime target. Like striped bass they seldom venture into deep water, spending their lives, instead, close to shore or in the inland waters such as Narragansett Bay, Peconic Bay, or the great inland waters behind the barrier beaches of New Jersey, Delaware and Maryland.

They are predators, as are all gamefish. But they are not the savage killers that tear through schools of bait, tearing and devouring the way bluefish do. They will herd bait at times, but this is not their way of life. Only twice have I seen them using wolfpack tactics on schools of bait—once off Delaware's Cape Henlopen last May, and then in September at Napeague Beach on outer Long Island.

Mostly they stay deep, capturing small fish and crabs near the bottom. Jetty fishermen from Sandy Hook to Ocean City, Md., catch them all season long by soaking chunks of mullet, worms, or crabs on bottom rigs. Others cast bucktail jigs or lead heads dressed with plastic tails of one sort or another. On one of my trips to Delaware a couple of years ago I bought a dozen brightly-colored plastic grubs, rigged them on jigs designed to carry bucktail, and outfished my New England companions who were using regular bucktail jigs.

The standard method is to fish a jig close to the bottom. Plain bucktail jigs work well, but if they are sweetened with a strip of fish belly, pork rind, or squid their effectiveness is improved. Some like a shrimp or sea worm impaled on the hook.

Live or cut mullet works as well as anything for bait fishermen. Live killies will take them, and dead or cut silversides, spearing or sand eels, are natural baits. Weaks will seldom pass up a hook baited with shrimp, and small crabs will interest them as well.

Weaks have formidable teeth, a pair of needle-like eye teeth that can puncture the unwary fisherman's skin. While weaks are not as bloodthirsty as bluefish, one would do well to avoid those teeth.

In the fall the larger fish move south first, with the smaller ones following. By October they are gone from Southern New England. They move south quickly once they start, deserting Long Island and New Jersey in October, leaving a few stragglers to be caught by late season fishermen, and lingering only briefly in Delaware and Maryland. A few are taken from Jersey jetties as late as November.

FLUKE

Half a dozen years ago fishermen were bemoaning the disappearance of the fluke, and marine biologists were coming up with reasons for their disappearance. In 1975 fishermen from Cape Cod to Assateague were wondering what to do with all of them.

Like the bluefish and weakfish, fluke appeared in 1975 in numbers that delighted fishermen. Back in the 1960's fluke virtually disappeared from Southern New England and thinned out along the rest of

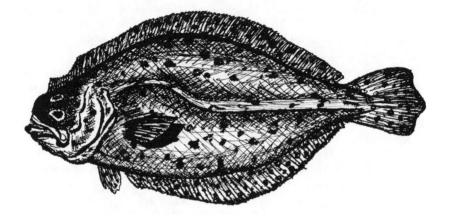

the coast. For as long as I could remember, it had always been possible to take a couple of dozen mummies out on the Point Jude breakwater or the wall at Sakonnet and come back with enough fluke fillets for a few meals. Suddenly the picture changed.

In 1972 a few reappeared, a year later they were back in greater numbers, and since then the population has been back to normal. Last year was equal to some of the best years of the 1950's along the Southern New England Coast.

But it has been along the Long Island and New Jersey coasts where you will find the real action. All summer long party boats and private craft returned to ports such as Montauk and Captree on Long Island, and Brielle in New Jersey, loaded with fluke. Many of the fish taken by boat fishermen off Long Island were under the state's 14 inch limit and had to be returned to the water. Yet there were enough keepers to satisfy every one. Beach and jetty fishermen did better in this respect; most of their fish were keepers. Most of the shorts came from the inland waters.

As the water cooled in the fall the numbers decreased, but the size of those taken more than made up for it. Several more than 20 pounds were taken, one a 22 pounder that will probably qualify as a new rod and reel record.

Fluke do not migrate to the south in the winter. They simply move offshore to deeper water. You can expect them to return when the water temperature reaches the low sixties, but they are not very active below 65 degrees. Between 65 and 75 is their preferred temperature range. If the water warms much above 75 they begin to move off toward deeper and cooler water.

I caught my first fluke last year at the Ocean City, Maryland inlet during the second week in May. At that time fishermen had been taking them for about a week. They can be expected in New Jersey's inshore waters toward the middle of May, Long Island fishermen get them about the same time, and New Englanders see them in early June. These fish are rarely found north of Cape Cod.

The shallow inland bays of Maryland, Delaware, New Jersey, and Long Island get them before surf fishermen get a crack at them because those waters warm up first.

Fluke feed almost exclusively on smaller fish, although they will take worms, clams, small squid, and small eels. They like their bait moving and will chase a trolled, drifted or reeled bait or lure willingly. While scorned by some surf purists as unworthy opponents (fluke are not flashy fighters), they are nevertheless abundant. These fish are easy to fillet and their white flesh keeps well in the freezer.

Fluke rarely take plugs. This is probably because, first of all, many salt water plugs are too large to interest an average fluke and, secondly, few plugs run deep enough to reach their normal feeding level. (I say normal feeding zone because, while they are bottom dwellers, I have seen them actually jumping and taking surface bait. This is rare, however.)

But they will take bucktail or plastic tail jigs, especially if the jig is sweetened with some natural bait. A strip of fluke belly on a bucktail jig is the most effective lure I've found. Mullet, preferably live, but also dead or chunked, find favor with fluke. Mummies are a standard bait in New England waters. Strips of squid are often used, but I have never found this to be as effective as fish of almost any kind.

Few fluke remain in New England shore waters after Labor Day. Long Island and New Jersey fishermen catch them through the end of the month, and Maryland and Delaware fishermen score until early October.

TAUTOG

Of all the species surf fishermen encounter, the tautog seems to be the only one that never fluctuates in abundance. They are always there, grubbing among the rocks for their sustenance, their only concern to find enough crustaceans or mollusks to satisfy their appetites. They are not endangered by commercial fishing since the only practical way to harvest them is with hook and line. Nets could never find them in their rocky environment.

Tautog migrate short distances each year from their offshore winter homes to esturine waters where they spawn in the spring, then to ocean front rocks for the summer, and then in late fall back to their winter homes.

Inshore fishermen begin to take them in bays and tidal rivers when the water temperature rises above 50 degrees. By the time the water has reached 60 degrees they are gone from the spawning ground and are hunting their food along the ocean front in rock piles and jetties. They remain there until the water temperature falls back into the low sixties and high fifties. Then they move off to deeper water. New England fishermen catch them into November from rocky shorelines. They linger close to shore well into November farther south.

Tautog are rarely, if ever, found over sandy bottom. Those creatures they feed on, crabs and shellfish which make up most of their diet, are found in and around rocks. So this is where tautog make their homes. More bottom rigs are lost by fishing for tautog than any other fish.

While they are not school fish they do congregate in small areas. Often a fisherman in one spot will be catching them regularly while another only a short distance away will be getting skunked. Mark well the spot where you get your first bite, for that may be right where the fish are.

I suspect if it were not for the jetties, New Jersey would have little tautog fishing. Jersey jetty fishermen take them in great numbers from rockpiles all along the coast and in inlets. The north jetty at Barnegat probably produces the heaviest tautog fishing. Delaware and Maryland also have tautog wherever there are rocks.

Northern fish, from my observation, run larger than those caught in the southern end of the range. Eight pounders are common in Rhode Island and Massachusetts and a 12 pounder is not an eyebrow raiser. However the world's all-tackle record, 21 pounds 6 ounces, was caught off Cape May, New Jersey. A 21 pound second-place tautog was caught in Jamestown, Rhode Island.

No-nonsense tackle is a must when fishing for these muscular and stubborn rock dwellers. Once hooked, a tautog turns his tail up and digs for the rocks. It takes a beefy rod and a strong line to stop him. If he makes it, considerable persuasion is needed to get him out.

Tautog take worms readily, but these are poor bait because water that holds tautog is invariably infested with cunners, those sharp-toothed bait stealers (and smaller relatives of tautog, by the way). Crabs also can clean a soft bait from a hook within seconds. Crabs are by far the best bait. Fished whole with just the claws removed, they are less vulnerable to attack by the bait stealers. Halved or quartered they are more attractive as bait, but are more susceptible to the teeth of cunners. Soft-shelled clams make good baits as well. The hook can be inserted through the tough snout with the shell crushed, but left on the clam. Tautog are perfectly willing to take the shell along with the meat.

Skimmer and razor clams will be taken by tautog, but here again the meat is favored by the cunners and crabs. Don't bother to float your bait above bottom with a cork, since the cunners feed at whatever level food is to be found.

A deadly bait is a couple of sand bugs threaded on a hook. These have the added advantage of being readily available on the beach beside the breakwater. On many beaches it is a simple task to gather enough for a fishing trip in a few minutes.

Either baked, filleted, or fried—tautog is the favorite of many a seafood gourmet. When filleting, watch out for a row of bones in the flesh along the side. They can be cut out with a sharp knife without wasting much good meat. Poach the fillets, let them cool, add mayonnaise, chopped onion, celery, and a little green pepper for a tasty salad.

Tautog range north of Cape Cod all along the Massachusetts north shore and into Maine, but they are scarcer in the northern end of New England. They are also taken off New Jersey by winter fishermen who find them off shore in deep water during the cold months.

Section 5

The Terrain

A tropical storm had delivered a glancing blow to the southern New England coast the day before which left an aftermath of high surf. The heavy ground swell rolled in, steepening as the waves began to trip over the shallow bottom and set up a rolling barrage along the beach. A few of us had gathered to test the theory that striped bass are partial to white water.

They were. Out where the late afternoon sun glinted on the breakers, school bass were greedily gulping our popping plugs.

One of our number that day was a young fellow from western Massachusetts, a personable lad who had expressed an interest in surf fishing. This was his first experience in fishing the Big Water. All his previous fishing had been done in the lakes and streams of the Berkshire Hills. But he caught on quickly. Before long his plug was landing alongside ours out in productive water.

He was about to get his baptism.

I was standing directly in back of him, unhooking a fish, while he was working on his first fish and wasn't far from having it beaten.

Now, out on the friendly shores of Lake Pontoosuc or Cheshire Reservoir, it's a simple enough matter to wade out to meet your fish, landing net in hand. But here there were six-foot breakers that were crashing to shore. Surf men make it a practice to back up the beach and let the waves boost the fish onto the beach where it can be grabbed before the next wave washes in. Unfortunately no one had thought to explain this to my companion.

He began edging towards the water. I shouted at him to be careful and then bent to the task of disengaging the treble hooks from the jaws of my fish. When I looked up again he was on the verge of being zapped by quite a few tons of green water. The wave broke before it hit him. Which was a piece of luck. If it had broken over him he might never have seen Lake Pontoosuc again.

I dropped my rod and reel in the sand which shows how urgent I considered the situation to be. Cleaning sand out of a reel is as pleasurable as changing a tire on the freeway. Then I raced toward the water.

The wash from the breaking wave, waist deep, toppled and buried him. His body hurtled into mine, at which point I joined him in that gritty, cold, green and white turbulence.

We were under water for not more than a few seconds, but a few seconds spent with your face pressed into the sand while the backwash is trying to suck you out to where the next wave can finish the job is very unpleasant.

We were tangled together like a couple of wrestlers. My fingers were buried to the knuckles in beach sand trying to hold us from being washed out. Somehow we held on until the backwash drained away. Somebody helped me drag him up the beach. Outside of having his breath knocked out he wasn't hurt. Once he got the water out of his waders and the sand out of his mouth, he was ready to go at it again. Somehow he had managed to hang onto the rod (for which I was thankful, since it was one of mine). The reel was operative again after field stripping and cleaning. Lord knows what happened to the fish. He's probably still laughing.

A man doesn't need many experiences like that to teach him the power of the surf. I have seen half a dozen men go in over the course of the years. All of them came out, but not everybody who goes in is that lucky. Some are still in there.

We will be dealing with three types of surf terrain in this book — sandy beaches, rocky shores, and jetties. Each demands respect. All can be productive when you learn how to fish them.

SANDY BEACHES

Sand beaches can be delightful places on those July days when the sun is melting the pavement back in the city. But when a two-day northeaster is driving mountains of gray water against the shore the delight is replaced by awesome din and fury. When a storm out at sea births a heavy ground swell, those long, seemingly gentle rollers steepen, crest, and then tumble with terrifying force.

It is unusual for a man to be washed out to sea from a sand beach. I've never seen it happen, although I've heard of it. Such an act would require a heavy mixture of stupidity and bad luck. Many have been upset in the wash; countless fishermen have sloshed back to dry sand, their waders ballooned with cold sea water. But to actually get washed out to sea from a sand beach would take some doing.

Don't panic if it should happen to you.

Concentrate on staying afloat. If you're wearing parka and waders or boots, your first thought will be to shed them. However, shedding parka and waders while trying to keep afloat is a stunt best left to the talents of escape artists such as the late Houdini. The air trapped in your clothes will help keep you afloat for a while. With any kind of luck you won't be in the water very long.

You won't be swept out to sea by the tide. The tide runs parallel to a beach, not out from it. If you can stay afloat, the tide will move you along the beach to a point where you can eventually work your way to safety. Don't worry about undertow. Any undertow will be beneath you and will not affect you if you are floating.

Anthing floating is moved toward shore by the action of the waves. The water itself isn't moving until the waves break, at which point the water races toward shore, carrying you and other floating objects with it. If you get in a breaking wave you will be tossed around a bit and thumped, probably painfully, on the hard sand bottom. Paddle, crawl, roll, somehow move yourself toward shore while the wash is racing in; then stretch out as flat as you can with your head toward land, giving the backwash as little surface as possible to work against.

Getting knocked down by a wave is a terrifying experience to be sure, but most of the time the only consequences are a thorough soaking, maybe a bruise or two, and a soul-cleansing scare. People have been known to take up religion after being knocked down by a wave.

There's a simple formula for keeping out of trouble on the beach — common sense and respect for the elements. Use it and you won't have any trouble.

Not all sand beaches are alike. Some drop quickly into deep water. Waves break directly on the beach and close to shore. These are the most dangerous. Others are flat and shallow. Here the waves break farther out and the wash is shallow, slower moving, less likely to upset a wader. Others have offshore bars that break the first force of the waves. A deeper slough generally runs between the bar and the beach with the beach usually dropping off rather steeply into the slough.

On beaches that drop off swiftly and where there are no offshore bars to interfere with the waves, gamefish often move in close to search for bait. Charlestown Beach, Rhode Island; Sandy Hook, New Jersey; the beach at Shinnecock on Long Island; and much of the Delaware beaches are like this. At times the fish are found in the wash, so close that a normal cast will put your bait or lure in barren water. I've had stripers so close at Charlestown Beach it was necessary only to lob my lure a few feet to draw a strike.

The flat, shallow beaches (the town beach at Narragansett, R.I. and Whale Beach in South Jersey are a couple that come immediately to mind) are more difficult to fish. They are usually best fished with bait. The angler wades out as far as he can, casts, and then wades shoreward with his bail open or his reel in free spool. The productive water is usually a long cast away.

Where there are offshore bars it is usually a waste of time to fish when the tide is low. Gamefish willingly come close when high tide provides a passageway through a cut in the bar since bait of all kinds can be found in the calmer, deep water of the slough. Once the tide begins to ebb they begin to move out. Not even the promise of continued feasting will hold a wary striped bass inside the bar once the water starts to run out. I have caught fluke inside the bar at low tide, but have never seen a bass or blue trapped in the slough with the bar exposed and the cut closed off.

There are places where low water permits you to walk out on the bar and fish the deep water beyond. Normally you'll have some wading to do to get to the bar, and if you've got as much sense as a striper, you'll keep one eye on that cut you had to wade across. Make sure you get off before it fills to wader-top level.

Take Deep Hole at Matunuck, Rhode Island, for instance. There is a mussel shoal that runs out beside the hole providing casting access to deep water. When the tide is low, the bar is exposed. At half tide the water washes over your knees and it is time to get off because water will be filling a cut between the beach and the shoal. Surf

fishermen lounge on the beach at high tide waiting for it to drop enough to permit them to wade the cut. The first impatient venturers invariably ship water in their waders as do those who wait too long to get off.

New England anglers often have tides of six to eight feet to contend with. Seagulls doze on the warm, dry sands of the offshore bars at low tide. Six hours later those bars are covered with five feet of churning water. Farther south the tides are less marked. Long Island tides average about five feet, while Sandy Hook to Ocean City tides are from 3½ to 4½ feet.

Coastal anglers are well aware of the tides, how they affect fishing, and of the dangers associated with them. Visitors from sweetwater areas are not so attuned to the tidal cycle.

There were half a dozen of us casting from the mussel shoal at Matunuck that night, all but one experienced surf anglers. The exception was a pilgrim from Iowa or some such place, a cousin of Little Augie. Little Augie was a five foot two, hard-fishing beach regular. His cousin was a carbon copy, small and determined.

We had waded through the cut on the bottom of the incoming tide. For two hours or more we cast swimming plugs into the dark water without so much as a tap. Then the water lapping against our waders told us it was time to get back to dry land. Which we did, wading the cut with the water inches from our wader tops.

We were racking our rods and kicking off our waders when somebody noticed Augie's cousin wasn't with us. The thin light of a rising moon disclosed where he was, still out on the mussel shoal casting.

"I told him," Little Augie moaned. "I told him we were coming in. Guess he thought we were quitting because we weren't catching anything and decided to try a little longer."

Our shouts were drowned out by the sound of the surf. Somebody was going to have to go out and get him. Little Augie was climbing back into his waders. "I'll go; he's my cousin," Augie remarked in a manner that made it clear he wasn't particularly happy with that fact. But by now the water in the cut was too deep for Little Augie to wade. Real good waders generally come in larger sizes than Augie. He struggled back to shore.

Then we saw the pilgrim start back. We turned on our flashlights to guide him. The water on the mussel shoal was now over his knees. When he entered the cut it rose with each step until only his head and shoulders were showing, and he was doing an awkward version of the dog paddle. Somebody shoved a rod toward him. He grabbed it and was pulled to shore.

He wanted to know, shrilly, why nobody had told him about the tide. When you're fishing on an Iowa lake I suppose you can stand on a sand bar or shoal as long as you want. He apparently assumed the same would be true in the Atlantic Ocean. Nobody had thought to tell him otherwise.

Then he wanted to know if the tide would go back out some time in the near future. We told him it would, in about six hours. Then in six hours, he said, Little Augie could go out and find the rod and reel he had borrowed. He had been so concerned with the more pressing matter of getting back alive that he had just dropped it and left it there.

The whole affair soured Little Augie on fresh water fishermen. It had been his second best outfit that his cousin was using. We never saw it again.

Where do you fish when you come upon a strange section of beach, all of it looking very much the same?

Well, books tell us to visit the beach at low tide to read the exposed bottom configuration and then return at high tide and fish accordingly. Sound advice. Low tide will tell you where the bars and cuts and sloughs lie, enabling you to plan your campaign.

If you haven't had a chance to study the beach at low tide you can still read the signs at high tide although they will not be as clear. Watch where the waves are breaking. If there is an offshore bar, even though it is submerged, the waves will be tripping over it. Look for a break in the line of breakers. That's deep water and that's where the gamefish will be passing to enter the slough. If the waves are regathering after being interrupted by the bar, it means there is deeper water in a slough between the beach and the bar. This will be likely water to fish. If the water breaks at an offshore bar and then the waves continue to trip over themselves on the way into the beach, it is shallow water and probably not productive.

If you find the waves breaking right on the beach there is deep water close in and good fishing might be found almost any place along the shore. Look for places where the water is moving in different patterns, surging over a submerged rock, forming a rip behind a protruding finger of beach, anything.

Watch the gulls and terns. A flock of gulls sitting on the water may mean they are gathered in that spot because fish were feeding there and they are waiting for them to break again. If gulls are flying and hovering over one area, that's the place to watch—even if the gulls are not diving. If terns are swooping and picking up bait, gamefish may be after the bait also. If gulls and terns suddenly congregate, wheeling and diving, get there as fast as you can and get a cast out to the spot.

How gulls know where fish are going to break is a mystery. Countless times I've seen gulls sitting on the rocks suddenly take to wing and head for a spot where the water erupts with thrashing bass or blues. Or they will be scattered over acres of water, apparently flying aimlessly, only to gather the instant activity begins.

Of course they have the advantage of being high in the air where they can see underwater activity. Cape Cod fishermen sometimes pool money to rent a light plane which flies one of their number over the beach to spot schools of fish. The information is passed to the men on the beach by way of Citizen Band radio and beach buggies speed to the designated area.

If no birds are around, watch the water for swirls, or showers or baitfish breaking water. From your angle anything under water is difficult to see, but occasionally bait will be seen glinting in the breaking waves. I have seen beach buggies equipped with towers. While the buggy patrols, a fisherman equipped with polarized glasses and binoculars sits in the tower and scans the water. Dead or cut-up bait lying on the beach is a sign that bass or blues have recently been present. Sand eels or spearing flopping on the wet shingle means they were chased there by bigger fish.

On strange beaches, if no surf signs tell me where to fish, I use the Original Boyd Fishfinder Method. What I do is look for places where other fishermen have congregated. Sometimes they don't know any more than I do, but more often than not, among them are some knowledgeable local anglers.

Now, if you do move in on these people please be a gentleman about it. If you find people catching fish, don't crowd too close. Usually they're willing to accept another fisherman, even move over a bit to accommodate him if he's a decent sort of a fellow. But they will resent crowding, believe me.

Sandy beaches are often unstable unless the sands are anchored with jetties. Bottom configurations change annually. Winter storms pick up sand and move it from place to place, shelving deep water with new bars, scouring holes where bars once blocked the waves. Beach buggy fishermen returning to Cape Cod beaches in the spring often must find new routes because the water here has cut away the sand to the base of the dunes or has piled up sand to create new dunes.

In 1760 a lighthouse was built at Cape Henlopen in Delaware on a 50-foot-high knoll a quarter of a mile from the ocean. Back in the 1920's it tumbled into the sea. Between 1930 and 1939 Indian River Inlet in Delaware opened and closed seven times. It was finally stabilized with jetties. Innumerable cottages along Cape Cod's outer shore have been undermined as the sea ate into the land.

What you know about a beach this year may not be true next year. You may have to learn it all over again. Rocky shores are more stable. And they present different hazards, different fishing opportunities.

ROCKY SHORES

While sand beaches predominate on the North Atlantic Coast, there are sections where great ledges, exposed by tide and wind, guard the land. Most of the Maine coast is ledge, either granite that is from 150 to 500 million years old or metamorphic rock from 250 to 600 million years old. The Massachusetts North Shore is alternately sand and very old rock dating back to the pre-cambrian period up to 1,000 million years ago. Cape Cod is a sand spit that is changing. It will probably be eaten by the sea in some future century. The Southern Massachusetts shore is rock interspersed with beaches; most of the Rhode Island shoreline around the mouth of Narragansett Bay is granite while barrier beaches stretch along the south shore. Mantauk Point is an island of rock isolated at the end of a long sand spit. From Sandy Hook south the coast is barrier beach.

While the rock outcroppings present some fine surf fishing opportunities, they also present increased hazards. Extra caution should be exercised. A step too far in the wrong direction, a bit of carelessness in gauging how far up the rocks the waves are breaking, and you may be tumbled into waters you may not escape from alive.

I've fished the rocky shore of Rhode Island for three decades now, and there is one inflexible rule I've never broken. Never fish alone. If I go into that water I want somebody nearby. With help one stands a chance of getting out. Alone that chance is diminished to odds I don't care to think about.

The first and most important rule to observe when fishing the ledges is this: *Don't step on the black zone.* This zone is a dense growth of minute plants, mostly blue-green algae that never completely dries out. Some of these plants are enclosed in slimy sheathes to prevent them drying out between tides. Massed together these plants appear to be no more than a darker section of rock, but the surface is as slippery as anything you'll ever step on. Chains or creepers under your soles help, but you'd be better off by staying away.

Don't go out on the rocks until you've watched to see how high the highest waves are breaking. You may feel safe with the spray drenching you, but a sneak wave may come along and sweep the rock clean of everything on it, including you. Make sure you know which way the tide is running. An incoming tide can leave you uncomfortably marooned or forced to swim for safety.

Some ledge slopes gradually down to the water, some is broken up into huge boulders, some ledge rises and drops off precipitiously into the sea. If you go off any one of them with a high sea running only, you're in big trouble! Several years ago I interviewed a survivor of a small boat accident. There were three men on board when the boat lost power and drifted into the shore of rocky Gooseberry Island at Westport, Massachusetts. One man was washed overboard before the boat struck. The other two managed to stay with the boat and get ashore. They watched the man who had gone overboard dashed to death on the rocks. He didn't drown. He was literally beaten to death.

Anyone going into the ocean from these rocky shores in a high sea could suffer a similar fate. If the sea is calm you have a chance of getting out. I have seen three men go in along the Rhode Island shore and all of them got out. One slid from his perch into deep water while fighting a fish. A companion was close enough to shove a rod tip out to where the man could reach it, and they managed to pull him in. Another time a man went down the rocks to gaff a fish. He stepped on the slick algae, sat down, and slid on the seat of his waders into the water. He not only scrambled back, but brought the fish with him as well. The third time is worth telling in a little more detail.

Evening success on Long Island.

Tom Morrison was much younger then. He was fishing a place called Frenchman's Reef, a shoreline of ledge and broken rock just north of the mouth of Narrow River in Narragansett. On that October night the cove in front of him was filled with bass—big bass, and they were hitting his swimming plugs. He already had a 47 pounder and a number of smaller ones on the rocks in back of him when the big one hit.

Tom declares it was the biggest bass he's ever hooked, over 50 pounds, and I must believe him. He was fishing from a ledge that dropped off perhaps three or four feet to where the spent waves, already broken by the reef that stretches out to form one side of the cove, were surging gently. He had been landing his fish by beaching them at a tiny cobblestone beach beside the ledge.

After a time Tom had the big fish licked. It lay on its side in the water below him, spent and ready to be taken. Tom lit the light that hung around his neck to guide him from the rock to the beach. The light hit the bass which suddenly gave a lunge and snapped the line at the leader knot. For a brief moment the fish lay there exhausted.

That brief moment was long enough for Tom to make a decision. Whether he weighed the consequences before taking action isn't known. Afterward, he didn't remember.

What he did was toss his rod onto the bank in back of him and with no more preparation than that, jumped in after the fish. The water luckily was only about three feet deep, but Tom went all the way under. He came up, reached out, embraced the fish in a bear hug and the battle was rejoined.

What Tom remembers most about that brief, but violent struggle was the plug filled with treble hooks. It was still attached to the fish's jaw and the fish was swinging it like a drunken sailor with a broken beer bottle. Here he was in three feet of surging water, his arms wrapped around fifty or more pounds of fish that was armed with a plug full of treble hooks swinging inches from his face.

While Tom clutched mightily the fish began to slip through his arms. There was one chance. If he could get a hand in the fish's mouth and grab a handful of gills, he might just bring him in. But the fish had its mouth closed. Tom unwrapped one arm and punched his opponent in the mouth (on the side away from the plug, of course), but this fish had had one stern lesson on opening its mouth this night and was not about to do it again.

In the end the fish slipped free and swam off slowly into the dark ocean. Tom climbed out of the water, laid on the ground with his feet up against a rock to drain the water from his waders, tied on a new plug, and went back to fishing. But no more fifty pounders came his way that night.

As dangerous as these rocks are they are heavily fished because they offer fine fishing for stripers and blues which chase bait right up to the base of the rocks. Tautog also make their summer homes all along these shores.

Reading the water here is elementary. Any place there is clear water, that is water not foul with rocks, can be productive. Almost anywhere is a good starting point. Coves formed by reefs harbor food for gamefish. Jutting ledges and submerged rocks create tidal rips. Everywhere the water surges and boils as it trips over rocks and dashes against ledges.

This water attracts fish. Stripers in particular have an affinity for rocks; hence the name rockfish as applied in some southern waters. In fact those rocky ledges are probably the main reason for Rhode Island's reputation as a hot striper area.

Cobblestone beaches present still other problems. There aren't many beaches of this nature. Some of the shoreline around Montauk Point is cobblestone and there are several such beaches in Rhode Island and Massachusetts. Carpenter's Bar at Matunuck, R.I. is typical. One must walk out from 50 to 100 feet, depending on the tide, to reach fishable water. Every step over the jumble of head-size stones represents a potential sprained ankle.

JETTIES

Much that was said about fishing the rocky shorline can be said about fishing jetties. I don't know if anyone has ever bothered to count the jetties that bristle from the New Jersey shoreline. There are hundreds certainly, possibly thousands. They keep the fragile barrier beach from change, anchoring the sand.

Much jetty fishing is done on warm summer days by those wearing sneakers, dungarees and T shirts. The serious fishermen wearing boots equipped with creepers and parkas and rubber pants against the spray, invade the jetties in the pre-dawn darkness or after night has driven the crowds away. These are the sure-footed pros; the men who take their fishing seriously.

Some jetties sit high above the tides, wet only when storm seas toss spray upon them. Others are awash at high tide. Some have flat surfaces to provide easy walking. Others are no more than jumbles of rocks.

No matter what the nature of the jetty, one should watch to see if waves are breaking over it at any point before venturing out. And one should be aware of the stage of the tide. What looks like a secure fishing platform at low tide can be awash when the tide comes in. Blue-green algae also clings to jetty rocks that are covered at high

tide and exposed when the waters recede. This is why many experienced jetty jockies wear creepers.

If you have expectations of catching fish, you can't swing onto the
rocks with your rod. Bring a long-handled gaff. Never climb down the
rocks to get a fish. It isn't worth it. Those barnacle-encrusted rocks
can lacerate like many exposed nails. I saw a man go off the Point
Jude breakwater one day. He wore only sneakers and bathing suit
and started to climb down toward the water to free his line that had
jammed in the rocks below. When I suggested he might be better off
breaking the line, he grinned and said it didn't matter if he fell in.
He'd enjoy a little swim.

He got his swim and quite a bit he hadn't bargained for. He slipped
on the algae, got sliced by the barnacles as he slid into the water, and
was then thrown against the rocks by the waves several times before
we could get him out. His next stop was a hospital. There wasn't much
of his hide that wasn't lacerated.

Jetties that line inlets are particularly dangerous. The water in an
inlet is often moving swiftly. These narrow passages are the outlets
for large inland bay systems. On an outgoing tide a lot of water is trying to get out all at once. Fall into it and you won't be able to swim
against it.

Nevertheless jetties are excellent places to fish. They permit an
angler to reach water he could not reach from the beach itself, and
they provide homes for small creatures that attract larger fish. Inlets

are particularly good since the outgoing tide spreads a chum line of bait upon the ocean's waters, drawing gamefish. Stripers, fluke, weakfish, kings and even bluefish use the inlets regularly to visit the rich inshore waters behind the barrier beaches.

For many gamefish you won't need to make long casts from jetties since the jetties themselves are an attraction, and gamefish are drawn to them. If it's tautog you're after, the closer you can get to the base of the rocks the better your chances. For other gamefish — bass, blues, fluke and weakfish — cast into the eddy that forms on the downtide side of the end. That's where the baitfish will have congregated.

TIME AND TIDE

Whether you're fishing sand beach, ledge, or jetty the tide is your fishing clock. It moves in and out in cycles of slightly more than six hours, giving us two periods of high and two of low every 24 hours.

Tides can be commented on only in a general way. On beaches with offshore bars and sloughs, the top half of the tide is productive. That's when the water surging through the cuts in the bars brings gamefish into the sloughs to feed. As the water drops, the fish return to the safety of the open sea.

And on a flat, shallow beach, the flooding water gives a blanket of security to wary gamefish which find comfort in having plenty of water over them while they scrounge on the flats.

Yet high tide is not the best tide for fishing all beaches. On some a drop off is far from shore and can be reached only when the surf caster can wade out toward it. I know of one Long Island spot where a bed of rocks holds stripers and tautog. Only when the tide is low can a surf caster wade far enough to reach it with a cast. On some rocky beaches, shallow ledges, sparsly covered at high tide, are exposed by falling water. Careful fishermen can use them as casting platforms to reach productive water. I've mentioned Matunuck Beach where fishermen can reach a mussel bed only at low tide. There are other places where flooding water fills passageways that can be waded to only when the tide is out. Some who fish River Rock, a huge granite outcropping that guards Narrow River in Narragansett, R.I., wade out to it on a low tide and remain there until falling water permits them to return to dry land. Many breakwaters and jetties stand safe and dry at low water but are awash and untenable when the tide comes in.

In general, the top half of the tide provides the best fishing in many places. That same high tide cuts off many other places or makes them difficult to fish.

A flooding tide sets the table for feeding fish by activating many organisms that are inactive during periods of low water. But a dropping tide, as mentioned earlier, flushes the rich inland bays and tidal rivers into the ocean. At river mouths and inlets, ocean predators gather on a falling tide to reap the bounty.

Knowledge of which tide to fish in any locality comes only with experience. Bottom configuration and accessibility are the governing factors. Almost any bait shop carries area tide tables that will help you plan your fishing trips.

As to the time of day, fishermen are traditionally early risers. That doesn't necessarily mean early morning fishing is always best. I suspect much of the early rising has to do with getting in a longer fishing day, and never mind that if you get a late start you can make it up on the other end of the day. You'll probably stay later than you ought to anyway, no matter what time you start.

Yet there is merit to early rising since the dawn hours are often the magic ones—if not in terms of production, in terms of the enjoyment of watching new daylight scatter the night.

Striper fishermen often sandwich their fishing around the midday hours, hitting the beach at dawn and dusk and recuperating in between. Cape Cod beach buggy fishermen reverse the normal sequence of sleeping and waking hours, prowling the beaches in the hours of darkness and sleeping when the sun is shining. Stripers are more likely to venture into shallow water under the cover of darkness. Yet during the fall migration when schools of stripers are moving south along the coast, any time of day might find them storming the beaches.

Bluefish seem to show little preference for time of day. They feed when and where opportunity presents itself. A midday high tide will bring them into the beach as well as a dawn, dusk, or midnight flood. Weakfish also feed around the clock. Most are caught during the daylight hours simply because it is more convenient for most to fish at that time. I've caught them often when night plugging for school bass. Those who pursue fluke, tautog, or kingfish can keep regular hours. They are daylight feeders which will cooperate as readily at high noon as when the sun is burning off the morning mist. The tides rather than the time of day are the deciding factor.

PLAYING AND LANDING YOUR FISH

There's an element of luck involved in successfully playing and landing a fish in the surf, just as there is an element of luck involved in every phase of fishing. This involves some basic techniques. Plus the ability to keep your head. Buck fever is not unknown among surf fishermen.

The fact is that there are innumerable ways to lose a fish (more than I can list here) and innovative anglers are finding new ways to lose fish all the time. I've discovered a few myself. Most involve equipment failure or some other preventable cause. Leader knots let go, reel drags jam, knicked or frayed lines pop, hooks straighten or pull out of plugs, rods snap. Equipment failure happens to the most careful fishermen, but not as often as it happens to the careless.

Buying good equipment helps. Never try to save money on snaps, swivels, leaders, for instance, and inspect your rod guides and tips regularly. Tie your knots carefully and test them before casting. Discard a few feet of line after every trip, for those first few feet invariably pick up knicks and cuts and are subject to the greatest stress. Back off on your reel drag between trips. Drag washers under continuous pressure compress.

Hope that nothing goes wrong, but be assured it will. Murphy's Law applies in surf fishing . . . in fact it may have originated in surf fishing. You know Murphy's Law. It holds that if anything can possibly go wrong, it will, and at the worst possible moment. The worst possible moment, of course, is when that fish you've been looking for all those years is stretching your line like a banjo string.

Also be assured that you are more likely to lose a big fish than a small one. It stands to reason. The size and strength of a big fish prolongs the battle, puts a greater strain on the tackle and gives Murphy's Law greater opportunity to become operative.

You will also find that later when you are relating the story of this big fish that got away, there will be a non-fisherman in the group who will wait until you are finished, look around to be sure everyone is paying attention, wink, grin, and ask, "How come it's always the big one that gets away?" Then he'll roar with laughter, maybe even slap his thigh, having gotten off a real zinger, and probably say it again for the benefit of anybody who might have missed it the first time. There is one of these at every party. That's one reason I seldom associate with non-fishermen.

The cardinal rule in fighting a fish is to keep a tight line, which is not always as easy as you might think. Fish don't always run straight out when hooked. They might go parallel to the shore, make circles, even dash shoreward. Whatever happens, your job is to keep that line tight. A slack line makes it easier for the fish to throw the hook, particularly during a prolonged battle that wears hook holes. I have seen hooks drop from the mouths of beached fish. If the angler had permitted the line to go slack, the fish would have escaped.

Always check the drag on your reel before you start to fish. You want it tight enough so a big fish can take line before the leader knot pops under the strain, but tight enough so smaller fish can be handled without the fuss of losing and regaining line. Never tighten the drag during a battle unless you have permitted it to get so loose you can't handle a fish. As the fish shrinks the line on the spool, the tension increases without tightening. With a spinning reel, never turn the handle unless you are gaining line. Otherwise every turn will put a twist in the line.

Fight the fish with the rod pointing upward. Now he's fighting the spring of the rod, and he'll tire more quickly. When he jumps, momentarily lower your rod.

As for setting the hook, techniques vary according to the species of fish and whether you're using bait or lure. Generally, when a fish hits a lure, your move is to strike back immediately. On bluefish, which have hard mouths, it doesn't hurt to whack the hooks home a couple more times. Do that with a weakfish and you stand a good chance of tearing the hooks right out of the mouth. Single hook lures, by the way, hold better than trebles.

When bait fishing, the technique is somewhat different. A fish must be given time to get the bait in his mouth before the strike is delivered.

Bluefish are notorious for chopping baits. Anglers using live eels, bunker or herring frequently reel in neatly severed parts of fish when the blues are around. The only answer to that is a multiple hook rig with the stinger snelled on wire. The rig is easy enough to make. Just run a short length of wire from the hook and attach a second or stinger hook to that. When a bluefish hits, instead of chopping off the bait, it will find itself with that stinger hook in its jaws.

Stripers will run with an eel or bunker before trying to swallow it, so striking too soon may fail to set the hook. The technique is to let the fish run on free spool or with an open bail until the fish stops. When it starts to move again you can be reasonably sure he has it deep enough to set the hook. Sea worms, crabs, clams and so forth will be sucked in and the hook can be set immediately. Weakfish tend to pick up baits more tenderly. Hard strikes by the angler are out of order.

Tautog can be tricky. They have two sets of teeth — one set in front for picking up the food; one at the entrance to the throat for crushing shells. That first tap you feel will be the pick up. A strike then may not connect. When you feel the second tug, the hook will be well back in the mouth and your chance of burying the hook is more certain. Don't be afraid to sock hard. Tautog have leathery mouths and considerable pressure may be necessary to sink the hook past the barb. Once you hook a tautog, keep the pressure on. Otherwise he'll get back into the rocks and that will be the end of it.

More fish are lost at the point of being landed than at any other time. By the end of the fight hooks may have worn holes in jaws, there is less line between the fish and rod tip to absorb shock, weak links in terminal tackle have been under stress and can give way, and the fish may be in water so shallow it can use the solid ground for leverage.

Landing a fish on an open sand beach is relatively simple. Let the waves work for you. By now the fish is tired and the waves will move it toward shore. Reel when the fish is in an incoming wave, hold on, or even give back a little line if you have to when the back wash moves it the other way. Get the fish in the last wave and haul. When the wave recedes the fish will be flopping on the wet sand.

Some surf fishermen stay out in the water and use a hand gaff, particularly when the fish are small, and then simply string them on a stringer attached to their belts. I prefer not to do it that way. Maneuvering a fish into a gaffing distance is tricky and more subject to risk than beaching it. And there's one other problem; although it's not a likely one. Surf fishermen standing in the water attached to strings of fish, some of which may be bleeding, can attract sharks. I've never seen it happen, but I've heard stories about anglers trying to divest themselves of strings of fish as they struggle toward shore. I believe them because, as everybody knows, surf fishermen hardly ever lie.

Landing a fish from a rocky shore or a jetty can pose different problems. By habit, when I'm fishing from Rhode Island's rocky ledges I look around for a likely place to land a fish before I start. It might be a small cove or a shelf or even a narrow beach; any place where I can reach the fish without climbing down over the rocks.

A long-handled gaff is useful when fishing from ledges or jetties. Often the best way to land a big fish when jetty fishing is to walk it back to the beach and land it there.

What do you do with a fish once you've landed it? On a sandy beach it's best to bury your fish. Not only will it stay fresher, but it will be safe from gulls. I've seen unattended fish ruined by gulls.

It also helps you hide your success from those who would move in on your territory. Just be sure to mark the spot. I recall a 15 pound striper that was buried on Nauset Beach on Cape Cod one night and the grave marked with an empty beer can. But some joker moved the can, and since one piece of beach looks pretty much like every other, the angler spent more than two hours digging before he retrieved his fish. That was more than 30 years ago, so I guess it's safe to admit that I was the one to move the can.

If you're fishing from a ledge or jetty you can usually find a safe spot to store your fish among the rocks, but not if you're fishing the Cape Cod Canal. The rats that make their home in the rip rap will get them. Either tether them in the water or carry them up the bank. In any event, clean them and get them on ice as soon as possible for good eating.

Experience will teach you much more about playing and landing fish. Let's drop the subject and go on a trip along the Atlantic Coast.

Section 6

From Popham Beach to Assateague

Nobody, given a mere lifetime in which to do it, could ever hope to hit every likely spot on the North Atlantic Coast. This reminds me of the old gaffer soaking a slice of herring off the beach at Sandy Hook one fall day a few years ago. We talked a while of how everything is going to hell these days and how much better they were in the old days. His old days pre-dated mine by quite a few years by the way. I asked him if he had been surf fishing all his life. He said he didn't know.

"You don't know?" I remarked with surprise.

"Nope," he said, "I ain't lived all my life yet."

I don't know how many people live within easy driving distance of surf fishing on the North Atlantic Coast. Probably 30 or 40 million. Not all, thank Heaven, are inclined toward the eccentricity we call surf fishing. But a lot of them are.

Surprisingly, as one trods the sand or climbs breakwaters and jetties he meets many surfmen who live in places where the only salt water to be found is that used for gargling. The New Jersey and Delaware beaches are cluttered with Pennsylvanians facing a two and a half hour ride to get back home. Long Island beaches host many who make their homes in Upper New York State, and the Rhode Island and Massachusetts beaches have a fair percentage of fishermen from inland New England. Worcester, Massachusetts, for instance, almost 100 miles from the nearest beach, is the home of some of the hardest-fishing surf men to be found anywhere.

These inlanders are not just casual fishermen. They are people who regularly drive hundreds of miles from their inland homes in the hope that when they arrive the tide will be right, the surf will be running high, and the fish will be feeding inside the bar. So you don't have to live within the sound of the breakers to enjoy surf fishing; not with today's super highways and the free time available to many of us.

If you live in this elbow-to-elbow megalopolis that runs along the coastal states, good surf fishing is probably no more than a couple of hours driving time away. The problem comes in knowing just where to drive to. Here's where I can help you, because I've been there.

Not everywhere, certainly, but to enough places so that I can direct you to a beach or jetty reasonably close to your home. Being limited to one lifetime, a part of which must be spent working for a living, has prevented me from going all the places I'd like to go.

This business of working for a living isn't a deterrent to everyone. A few years ago a friend of mine was fishing Cape Cod beaches in September when he decided to follow the striper migration down the coast a ways. He ended up in Ocean City, Maryland, in November, broke. He managed to get his beach buggy home by driving alternate routes (not having the money to pay the tolls). When he got home he no longer had a wife or a job.

Being something less than a free spirit, I've had to limit my traveling to vacations and long weekends, but this has still permitted me to visit some of the finest surf fishing spots in the country.

This trip down the coast will be limited, first of all, to those places I've actually visited. I have no intention of reading some Chamber of Commerce or state tourist bureau brochure and passing that information along. You can do that yourself. Anyway, the people who write this material have been known to stray from objectivity from time to time.

There will be another limiting factor. Most fishermen don't own beach buggies, vehicles designed to drive over the sand. I don't own one, although I've logged a good many miles as a passenger. So I'll not, in most instances, be taking you places reachable only by beach buggy.

Along much of the coastline there are access points to the beach that permit a fisherman to reach good surf fishing within reasonable walking distance. Your definition of reasonable walking distance may differ from mine, of course. As the years pass my reasonable walking distance has been diminishing until now I'm much inclined to fish the water nearest the parking lot and leave the far beaches to those with four wheel drive or younger and stronger legs.

There is the matter of definition. Surf fishing means just that, fishing on the open ocean front where the waves break on the shore. There are thousands of inland salt water fishing holes along the coast—bays, river banks, bridges, piers and so forth—where you can catch the same ocean gamefish you catch in the surf. We'll not be concerned with those.

Before we set out, bear in mind that most of these places were visited only in spring or fall, not during the summer months. Conditions may not be the same during June, July, and August when most folks take their vacations. Beaches then are jammed with people.

Resort areas are crowded, motels and restaurants jack up their prices, and local laws favoring the bathers keep surf fishermen off the beach. So, while I fish Southern New England waters near my home all summer, I do most of my traveling before Memorial Day and after Labor Day.

MAINE

Maine has an almost endless coastline, made up largely of granite ledge that protrudes into the sea in a series of craggy capes and then retreats far inland to form deep, narrow coves and harbors. Surf fishing is mostly unexploited. Clem Walton, a marine biologist with the State Department of Sea and Shore Fisheries, and self-styled top rod on the coast has an explanation for this.

Courtesy of the Maine Department of Commerce and Industry

"Maine people," he told me half a dozen years ago, "are oriented toward fresh water sport fishing. They're interested in trout and salmon. They don't even seem to care that they've got such great surf fishing right here in front of them." He noted that vacationists are also more often interested in the state's trout and salmon fishing which is promoted by Maine's interest in tourism.

When I fished with Clem, surf fishing in Maine was limited almost exclusively to striped bass, although a few other species such as pollock, mackerel, and winter flounder are sometimes caught from the shore. Since then bluefish have moved in to give the sport a new dimension.

One of the most popular spots for surf fishermen along the middle Maine coast is Popham Beach at the mouth of the Kennebec River, a river that holds a large summer population of stripers and, Clem tells me, a winter population as well. Popham beach is easily reached by taking Route 209 south from Route 1 at Bath. An out-going tide, with the tea-colored river water emptying into the ocean is an ideal time to fish. Natives tie on three or four ounce sinkers, even heavier at times, to hold water in the rushing current, and bait with worms or cut mackerel. Around the point on the ocean side, pluggers work the surf with deep-running plugs or heavy bucktail jigs. Surface poppers will take both bass and blues when bait is present and the game fish are chasing it.

Popham beach regularly produces some of the largest stripers taken in Maine, a state not noted for the size of the bass that summer close to its shores. It was there in 1969 that I earned a shoulder patch and a certificate of membership in the Maine Tackle Busters Club with a 20 pound striper that fell to a flourescent orange deep-running plug. It was one of the very few times in a lifetime of fishing that I have ever been recognized for anything, although I do believe I hold the record for fishing the most consecutive hours with a hole in my waders.

This area has another plus. It is not heavily populated with bathers in the summer months. At least it wasn't the times I fished it.

Further down the coast, south of Portland, is Old Orchard Beach, another easy-to-reach and popular surf fishing spot. You can get there by turning off Route 95 at Route 5 at Saco. Here again cut mackerel and worms are the favored baits. Stripers I've caught here run smaller on the average than those caught at Popham Beach.

Almost any spot along the beach can be good, but my favorite spot is a rock about a half mile west of the pier. I arrived at my motel one Friday night a couple of years ago, walked out on the beach before going to dinner just to see what was happening, and found a pair of local fishermen scoring on cut mackerel right in front of the motel. I had a late supper that night. Old Orchard is a popular resort area; so don't plan any fishing trips there during the tourist season.

A ride through Biddeford, across the Saco River on Route 208, will take you to Biddeford Pool which is not a pool at all, but a peninsula that runs out the south side of the Saco River. The river itself is heavily fished by boatmen who drift herring in the spring and troll worms and spinner rigs all summer. Plug fishing comes into its own in the early fall.

The author hauls in a school bass at Biddeford Pool, Maine.

Biddeford Pool has a crescent-shaped sand beach anchored at one end by a rocky point and interspersed with ledges. It was here that I had my worst fright in three decades of surf fishing.

The beach that misty September morning was lined with fishermen bottom fishing, mostly with worms. I was closest to a rock ledge that ran out perhaps 50 feet into the water on my left. A friend who would have nothing to do with bait fishing had been off to my left, fishing a small blue popping plug. He came back through the mist after about a half hour. I called, "Anything doing over there?"

"Nothing," he called back. Then, when he was closer, whispered "Put that damned bottom outfit away and get your small plugging rod. I've got half a dozen fish on the beach already." I set my rod in my sandspike, grabbed my small plugging rod and followed him.

The surf that morning was light. I waded out to where the low swell lapped my hips and prepared to make my first cast. Suddenly a huge shape resembling some species of man-eating shark appeared out of deep water and headed straight for me. This was long before the movie "Jaws" appeared to panic ocean bathers, but I needed no such suggestion to picture those teeth.

Well, you can't run very well when you're up to your hips in salt water, and my legs weren't getting the message that all I wanted out of life at the moment was to get the hell out of there.

The huge shape undulated swiftly toward me and then, just as those jagged teeth were about to rip through my flesh, the whiskered, comical face of a seal broke through the surface and stared at me briefly. Then the creature whirled and disappeared, leaving me to redistribute the internal organs that had jumped from their assigned positions.

The day got better after that. My small, blue popping plug delivered, and I caught four school stripers before the sun burned off the mist and the fish left for other parts. None of the worm fishermen got a fish as far as I know.

There are many, many more surf fishing opportunities along the Maine Coast. One year, taking a sweetwater vacation, I found the trout and salmon fishing slow and drove to the coast at Mt. Desert Island where, using a fresh-water spinning rod and casting a small spoon from the rocks, I caught dozens of scrappy one to two pound pollock. These fish are every bit as scrappy as their more glamorous and more highly publicized surf colleagues, stripers and blues.

I'll never have the time to do more than sample Maine's surf fishing opportunities. Clem Walton, who not only fishes on his own time, but uses his job as an excuse to fish as well, admits he'll never cover it all. So the best thing you can do when you're in Maine is check with some local fishermen or tackle shop and take off from there.

That stripers are among the most popular marine gamefish is shown by a creel census taken by the state in the 1960's. This showed striped bass to be second only to cod in numbers of fish caught. While there was no breakdown showing percentages of shore-caught fish versus boat-caught fish, certainly many of the stripers must have been caught from shore. Interestingly enough, bluefish appeared only once in the five year study. That was in 1962 when two were recorded. A creel census taken now would show a marked increase in bluefish.

MASSACHUSETTS

Coming down the coast into Massachusetts (New Hampshire has a short stretch of shoreline and there is surf fishing available, but I have never sampled it) we come to Plum Island, a purely delightful place. Most of Plum Island is a national wildlife refuge under the jurisdiction of the U.S. Fish and Wildlife Service.

The Parker River Wildlife Refuge, which encompasses the lower two thirds of the island, is open to fishermen at all times. There is frequent and easy access to the beach and the miles of open beach offer unlimited surf fishing opportunities.

You reach Plum Island by turning off Route 95 at Newburyport, Massachusetts, and following Water Street to the Plum Island Turnpike. When you reach Sunset Boulevard, and don't let the term "boulevard" fool you, turn right and you'll come to the entrance of the Parker River Wildlife Refuge.

There is no charge for entering, and you may stay and fish all night with a permit, also free. The rules permit only fishermen on the beach at night, so if it's romance instead of fishing you've got in mind, better have a couple of fishing rods with you. No rods, out you go. Beach buggies are also permitted around the clock but you don't really need one. You can reach plenty of good fishing water on foot.

A single road bisects the six and a half mile refuge which averages something less than a half mile in width. There are parking areas and over-the-dunes access by foot at regular intervals, 15 of them in fact, and from any parking lot the beach is no more than 100 yards away. A policy of limiting the number of cars to the number of parking places means that at no time will you be overcrowded. Access to the refuge is limited to the Sunset Boulevard entrance, walking in on the beach is prohibited.

As to the fishing, I've had my best luck at the southern tip of the island. At Parking Lot 15 there is a clump of rocks that seems to attract gamefish. The very southern tip of the island, not under federal control, incidentally, but accessible to fishermen, is the northern side of a wide inlet that admits ocean water to the marshes and rivers that extend inland in back of the island. The inland waters teem with aquatic life that attracts gamefish.

I would hesitate to suggest any single spot along the beach. Like any sandy beach it changes each year as tides and storms shift the sands. Several years ago on a June morning I took half a dozen bass from a small rip that appeared behind a bar that extended from the beach. When I returned in September the bar was gone.

Stripers arrive at Plum Island about mid-May, but the best fishing does not begin until two weeks later. Fishing is best throughout June, then falls off during the summer months. However, Plum Island, like many other areas north of Cape Cod, is now visited by bluefish which have taken up some of the summer slack. But this is not dependable fishing. The blues come in to shore at irregular intervals, stay in for a few minutes or a couple of days, and then vanish until they return again.

September sees the bass and blues gathering for the fall migration. From then until mid-October is fast fishing. Some bass winter over in the Merrimac River and the Parker River, and I understand some people fish for them. Preferred bait for fishing the surf is worms, cut mackerel, cut herring, or squid. Bait fishing is more productive in the spring, nighttime eeling brings best results during midsummer, and a wide variety of plugs are effective when the water begins to cool.

Winter doesn't bring an end to surf fishing on Plum Island, although only the hardiest partake of it. Cod move close to the beaches during the cold months under the cover of darkness and there is a dedicated cadre of weather-proof anglers who cast clams or cut bait by the light of gasoline lanterns. They stick their rods in sand spikes and wait until a cod bites or hypothermia sets in — whichever comes first. Having managed to stay at least on the borderline of sanity over the years, I have never tried this kind of fishing.

The Plum Island area is the home of one of the most unique and hardest-fishing clubs along the coast. The Light Liners Inc. is a club dedicated to light line marine fishing. Its members regularly take out-sized bass and blues on four and six pound test line. The club also conducts an annual clean-up of the island's beaches.

Our next stop is the single exception to the definition of the term "surf fishing". Instead of the high surf beating against the shore here, we have a wide, seven-mile-long ditch filled with boiling, swirling water that races through at a five knot clip. It's the Cape Cod Canal. This is included because it is readily accessible. Any part of it can be reached in an easy walk. I have first-hand knowledge of it, and it does produce fish. There isn't a month of the year when you can't catch something in it. The warm weather brings in stripers, blues, tautog, and mackerel—while winter flounder are thick in the spring and fall. Cod and pollock are taken all winter.

Striper fishing in the Canal starts early in the season when the big bass arrive to chase the herring that swarm through on their spring spawning run. The herring gather in countless numbers at the mouth of a small river that enters the canal about a mile or so south of the Sagamore Bridge. Fishermen dip them out in long-handled nets and keep them alive in small bait cars or cages tied to the bank. They fish them live, hooking them through the mouth or back and casting them so they will drift with the current. Some walk along the bank with the reel in free spool or the bail open, keeping pace with the current. Others simply cast them into the current and let them swim freely until the tide swings them back close to shore.

By June, when the herring run has petered out, the small bass appear, followed by bluefish. From then on plugs, bucktail jigs, and the time-honored eelskin rigs are most effective.

Except during the early-season herring run, virtually all Canal fishing is done at night or early morning hours, although when bass and blues are moving through in the fall, fishing can be good any time of day or night.

To anyone who is accustomed to the regular, six hour tidal cycle, the Canal's tides are uncontrolled madness. The ditch connects two Bay systems, Cape Cod Bay on the easterly end and Buzzard's Bay on the west. There is about a three-hour difference in the tides at either end.

Here's just an example: Reading from a day on one season's tide chart, we find that slack water, when the tide turned from west to east, occurred at 2:31 a.m. Slack water occurs at the same time the entire length of the canal. Now, on that same day, high tide at the west end was at 1:09 a.m., about an hour and a half before the turn while high tide at the east end was at 4:21 a.m., almost two hours after the turn and about three hours after high tide at the west end.

Confusing? No wonder Cape Cod Canal fish act strangely.

What they do is move with the tides. Canal regulars chase up and down the banks stopping here now, there then to hit spots they know should hold fish at specific stages of specific tides. Only one who has fished the Canal for years partakes of this madness. Others station themselves in favorite spots and let the fish come to them. Still others patrol the banks looking for breaking fish or schools of bait. Some prefer westerly tides; some prefer easterly tides. When the fish are moving south in the fall, anglers argue whether the westerly running tide is best because it brings migrating fish from Cape Cod Bay. The easterly running tide holds the fish in the Canal while they wait for the tide to turn. Take your choice.

Or do as I usually do. Stop in at the Red Top Bait and Tackle Shop or Cape Cod Charlie's or Caldara's and ask the man for advice.

Because of the rocky nature of the bottom and the swift current, bait fishing is not popular except in rare instances. In this plug-oriented territory most fishermen arm themselves with artificials. Yet I have seen times when only bait would do, and it was one of those times that got me the biggest striper I've yet to catch from that foolish ditch.

The Preacher and I arrived at the east end of the Canal just as the sun was poking its edge over Cape Cod to find the bank lined with fishermen. Most had their rods propped in the rocks and their lines angling out into the water. Two were fighting fish and one was administering the last rites to a thrashing ten pound blue with a short club.

They were, it developed, catching bluefish by fishing cut mackerel on the bottom. The blues were having nothing else. The plugs and bucktail jigs the Preacher and I threw at them were ignored. "What we've got to do," I said finally, "is go and get some mackerel and some bottom rigs. It's the only way we're going to get any fish out of here today."

The Preacher agreed, but reluctantly. He was a plug fisherman and the thought of sitting on the bank soaking a piece of cut bait was not his idea of fishing. Nevertheless, if he were to have baked stuffed bluefish for Sunday dinner, this was the only way he was going to get it.

So we racked our rods and made a tour of the tackle and bait shops. There wasn't mackerel to be had. We finally settled for a box of frozen squid. But back at the Canal the fishing was about over. The sun was high in the sky, the tide had turned and most of the fishermen were shouldering their rods and hauling great strings of bluefish, many of them a dozen pounds or better, up the bank.

"A waste of time," the Preacher said. "Throw that squid away and let's go home." But I had just paid a buck for that squid, and anyone whose grandparents came from Paisley, Scotland, does not throw a buck's worth of squid in the water—not unless there's a hook in it. The Preacher permitted himself to be persuaded to give it a try.

We cast our baits, propped our rods in the rocks and sat a while. Pretty soon the Preacher, a nervous individual to whom sitting still is a form of torture, decided to walk back along the bank to see if anyone was still scoring.

He was no sooner out of sight than his rod tip dipped. I shouted, but he was too far away to hear. Later he accused me of shouting under my breath and threatened to denounce me from the pulpit. He never did, but he remains unconvinced. There was nothing else to do but pick up his rod and land a 21 pound striped bass. You never saw a madder preacher in your life.

I went to a supermarket that afternoon and bought a couple of mackerel. The next morning I returned to the same spot. The preacher couldn't go—it being a Sunday, his day of work. The blues were still there, but the only one catching them was a fellow who had some cut herring. The rest of us caught dogfish.

That's the way the Canal is. Few can figure it out. I found a school of breaking fish one night just to the east of the Scusset Fish Pier on the east end. They were fairly small fish, a couple of pounds, and they were chasing small bait close to the shore. I tried everything down to a mackerel jig, but couldn't get a hit. I thought at first they might be small blues; then decided they were pollock. I found out when several swam between me and the shore. I scooped and a two pound cod flopped on the rocks. A cod chasing bait like a blue? Crazy! Never heard of such a thing except in the Cape Cod Canal.

The fishing at either end can be quite different because the Cape Cod Bay end is somewhat colder than the Buzzard's Bay end. Such cold water fish as cod, pollock and mackerel are taken off the east end while weakfish, scup and summer flounder are in Buzzard's Bay.

The Canal is easy to reach, just follow Route 3 from Boston or Route 195 from Providence or New Bedford. Roads run along either side and there are many parking places from which you can walk in. Some of the bait shops have maps showing the best fishing spots. The Canal is maintained by the Army Corps of Engineers which maintains a hardtop service road on either side, but these roads are off limits to private vehicles. Bicycles are permitted, however, and some rig their bikes with rod racks and pedal the service roads looking for signs of feeding fish.

A word of warning. The rip rap that lines the Canal can be hazardous. Not only are the stones prone to roll when you step on them, those covered at high tide are slippery as well. The lower stones are bearded with rockweed.

And the rip rap is infested with rats. Sit quietly under one of the street lights that line the service roads on any night and before long you will see them scurrying around picking up scraps of lunches and bait left by fishermen and scrounging for dead fish and crabs and anything else edible tossed up by the tide. I've never heard of anyone being bitten by one, but I never met anybody who likes rats, either.

If it's the high surf you want, the Outer Cape has it and plenty of it—although a good part of it can be reached only by beach buggy. Race Point at the very tip of Cape Cod, for instance, a storied fishing spot, is too far to walk to, and the Chatham Inlet at the southern tip of Nauset Beach can be reached only by beach buggy or boat. But there are beaches within foot-slogging distance from the parking lot.

I'll tell you about the ones I consider best. My personal favorite is Head of the Meadow Beach in Truro, six miles this side of Province-town (call it P Town if you want to sound like a native).

There are now two large parking lots there, one controlled by the town of Truro and the other a part of the National Seashore. During the bathing season, parking in the town lot is by resident permit only. There is a fee for entering the National Seashore lot. But after Labor Day you can park without permit or charge. This is when the best fishing is to be found anyway.

Offshore sand bars break the surf all along this stretch of shore, but there are gaps that provide passage for gamefish which come in with the tide to feed the rich sloughs between the bars and the beach.

In the spring, usually early June, school bass hit this area. This is the time to cast sea worms out to the cuts and the sloughs on the top of the tide. Later larger fish appear and fishermen switch to squid, cut mackerel, or herring or eels.

In the fall and on summer nights this is big bass water. And big bluefish water, too. Most fishermen now are pluggers, casting swimming plugs into the night tides and switching to top water poppers after the sun comes up. Metal lures are deadly when the gamefish are herding bait.

A mile or so to the south is Highland Light where a high bluff looks down over long stretches of beach. The marine terrain here is much like it is at Head of the Meadow—offshore bars, cuts and cloughs. I have sometimes fished the beach between the two by leaving one car at Highland Light, driving to Head of the Meadow and fishing back.

In some places here the beach drops quickly into the deep water of the sloughs and gamefish will crowd close to the beach, making long casts unnecessary. At low water it is possible to walk out on some of the bars and fish the deep water beyond.

The closest you can get by car to Race Point is Race Point Light. Park your car here and walk as far as you care to in either direction. You might find fish anywhere. Other access points to Outer Cape beaches are National Seashore beaches at Nauset Beach Lighthouse at North Eastham and the Cape Cod National Seashore Headquarters in Eastham. I haven't fished these places regularly, so I can't pass along much information. The Goose Hummock Bait Shop in

Orleans can help you. The town beach at Orleans is a part of famed Nauset Beach. A mile or so north of the town parking lot is Nauset Inlet if you don't mind the hike. Entrances to all these beaches from Route 6, the Mid Cape Highway, are clearly marked.

Since the mid 1970's striper fishing from the Outer Cape beaches has fallen off. There has been fair fishing in the spring, poor fishing all summer and usually a fall blitz at Nauset Beach at the end of September. Blue fishing has ranged from hot to non-existant.

I'll mention one more place on the Massachusetts Coast. It's Gooseberry Island, a barren, rock-bound few acres at the end of Route 88 in Westport, Mass.

There were summer cottages on the island until a hurricane removed them in the early 1950's. After that the state forbid any more building and let the causeway deteriorate. The causeway has now been repaired, and there is a parking lot on the island.

Gooseberry is an interesting place to fish. The west shore faces the prevailing southwest winds and the surf coming in grinds itself to death on jumbles of rocks. It's hard going, but it can be fished and is productive. I took both stripers and blues there in 1975 while Outer Cape anglers were drawing blanks.

You can leave your car in the parking lot and a ten minute walk will take you out to the best fishing water.

Gooseberry is uncluttered with bathers. Nearby Horseneck Beach takes care of them. In fact it's usually relatively clear of non-fishermen of any kind. There's nothing on the island but a couple of Coast Artillery towers left over from World War II. Bait fishing is impractical here; the jumbled rocks eat bottom rigs as you or I eat peanuts. It's plugging water.

Nearby Horseneck Beach also offers surf fishing after the bathers have left for the season. Toward the northern end of the beach where the Westport River empties into the sea is a prime spot for fluke. This is away from the main beach and is usually clear of bathers even in the summer season. Don't go all the way to where the beach turns the corner into the river. It's shallow water there. Try about 100 yards to the south near a rock pile and opposite a rock that looms out of the ocean a couple of hundred yards off shore. Don't be surprised if your bucktail jig or your bait is attacked by a bass or blue when fluke fishing. I've walked off this beach a few times with mixed strings of fluke, bass, and blues. One time an eight pound bonito grabbed my bucktail jig and gave me the frights. Bonito have absolutely no concern for the peace of mind of an angler. They tear off eight pound line by the yard.

One reason for this area's fine fishing is the Westport River with its far-flung system of marshes. I've never seen the mouth of the river when there wasn't bait present.

RHODE ISLAND

Going over into Rhode Island the first place we hit is Sakonnet Point, another rocky shoreline and a hot spot for tautog, fluke, stripers and blues. The fluke are taken off the breakwater at the point. Tautog inhabit the rocks and bass and blues feed in the surf.

You get to Sakonnet by turning off Route 195 in Fall River and heading south on Route 138. When you get to Tiverton take Route 77 south through some of the prettiest countryside you'll see anywhere.

Sakonnet is in Little Compton, a tiny town of ancient burial grounds, colonial houses and history. Its shoreline is mostly rocks. Access to the water is limited since much of the land is privately owned, but there is surf fishing available at Sakonnet Point and at Warren's Point a little to the east.

Newport, Rhode Island has some of the most spectacular shoreline scenery on the coast. The city's Ocean Drive runs along a shoreline of granite and slate ledges that provides casting platforms at the edge of a rollicking, churning surf. The waves crash over offshore rocks, regather and bust against shore ledges, throwing their spray high in the air. It's the kind of water striped bass and tautog love. Blues, too, visit this turmoil as they chase schools of bait.

Parking is limited along the drive to designated areas, but there are enough of them so you can fish much of the good water. Mansions built by 19th Century millionaires line some of the shoreline, blocking access to some of the shore.

Every year someone takes a step too far and goes into the water here. Most, but not all, come out alive. It's a mean coast at times, so be prudent.

Castle Hill, which anchors the westerly end of the drive where the ocean front turns the corner to enter the east passage of Narragansett Bay may be one of the best tautog holes anywhere. A high, granite bluff makes fishing here chancy. The tautog make it worthwhile.

To reach Newport leave Route 195 at Route 114 a few miles east of Providence and follow it all the way. There's a 30¢ toll at the Mt. Hope Bridge. If you're on the westerly side of Narragansett Bay and you want to get across without driving around through Providence, take Route 138 across the Jamestown Bridge and the Newport Bridge. The Jamestown Bridge is toll free, but the Newport Bridge will cost you two bucks. If you go this way, stop off at Beavertail on

Tautog from Castle Hill, Newport, Rhode Island

the southern tip of Jamestown. Fine tautog fishing and a favorite spot for bass and bluefish pluggers.

Across the mouth of Narragansett Bay is the Narragansett-Point Judith area, my home stomping grounds. It was here I caught my first fluke, my first bass, my first tautog, and my first blue. Want to hear about my first striped bass? You know some surf anglers fish for years before they catch their first striper. I caught mine ten minutes after I started.

Joe Tartorie was responsible. Joe and his wife, Rose, ran the Point Jude Bait Shop on Boston Neck Road in Narragansett. He was free with advice and information. Joe, by the way, was a pioneer at fishing the surf with a fly rod. He took fish up to 21 pounds by that method. And Rose was one of the first in the area to see the advantages of spinning tackle. In her day she put many a male fisherman to shame.

Anyway, Tom Morrison and I had been fishing for fluke and tautog off the Narragansett-Point Jude shoreline with moderate success. Now we wanted to try for stripers, but the stubby rods and narrow-spool reels we had didn't seem appropriate. Striper fishermen, we knew from having seen many, carried long split bamboo or Calcutta rods with wide-spool reels, wore waders and fished the high surf.

Joe asked us one day when we went in to buy bait, "How come you fellows aren't fishing for stripers?" We told him why. We didn't know how, didn't have the equipment, and furthermore didn't know where to go.

He told us where to go—the west wall of the Harbor of Refuge at Point Jude. He told us what to use—an eelskin rig; when to go—when there was a high tide about dawn; and how to do it. Just cast out and retrieve. Within ten minutes I had a three pound striper. Before I had the hook out, Tom had one too. That was the only one I caught that night. A couple of casts later I had a backlash, my nine thread linen line snapped, and I lost the only eelskin rig I had.

A ten pounder caught at the Sheep Pen just north of Point Jude.

For the rest of that season Tom and I caught fish regularly there and then. Over the winter months we built Calcutta rods, got better reels, and filled them with the new nylon squidding line. We stocked up on plugs, block tin and eelskin rigs, and started to fish the real surf, out where the big ones are. We'd had our schooling off the breakwater and now it was time to move up.

It was a couple of years before either of us caught another striper.

Of course if we'd had something like *Atlantic Surf Fishing* as a guide. . .

All right, back to the present. The Narragansett-Point Jude (Proper name Point Judith, but Point Jude sounds saltier) area has everything a surf fisherman could want, all in the space of a few miles. There is a tidal river entering the sea, an inlet into a huge salt pond, stretches of sandy beaches, rocky beaches, jetties, a point that protrudes into the ocean to intercept migrating fish, hard sand bottoms for fluke, rocky bottoms for tautog, rips and eddies for stripers and blues, and weakfish anywhere.

The coastline has been thoughtfully laid out so you fish with the prevailing southwest wind at your back or in your face. It's your choice. If the wind shifts you can shift. Access to the water is frequent; a beach buggy is unnecessary—for the whole area is fed by good roads. I don't know what more a surf fisherman could want.

Take Route 108 from Route 1 and drive directly to Point Judith Light. Park your car in the public parking area, shoulder your rod and try any place around the point. This is not easy fishing by any means. The ocean throws itself at a jumble of rocks at the foot of the retaining wall around the light and some rock-hopping under the fire of the waves is in order. On the southwesterly side of the light, a rocky shoal runs out from the shore. If the tide is not too high, and if the sea is not too heavy, you can wade out and fish some fine water.

Get in your car, drive back a quarter of a mile and turn left onto a private road that will take you out to the base of the east wall of the Point Jude breakwater. Not during the summer, though. Someone will try to collect a couple of bucks from you for parking. When you get out there, don't go out on the breakwater. Go down onto the rocky shore and fish the corner where the breakwater meets the shore. On an early morning high tide your chances of hooking a bass or blue are good.

Fish off the end of the breakwater with crabs for tautog. Fluke are on the sandy bottom on the inside in the summertime.

Now drive a half mile back to the next crossroad and take a right, pass a restaurant called Aunt Carrie's, and find a dirt road leading down to the shore. Plug along there for a while or bottom fish for tautog.

Go back to the main road and take a right. Now you're on Route 1A headed north. A half mile up the road, past the last street on the right that has houses on it is a pile of dirt blocking a dirt road. Park there and walk in about a hundred yards. Just to your right a couple of huge boulders surrounded by a court of surf-washed rocks stand off the beach. If the tide is high, cast out around these big boulders. If it is low, wade out and cast beyond. Try all along the rocky beach to the right as far as a breakwater a couple of hundreds yards away.

The next stop is Scarborough State Beach, headquarters for the state's teeny bopper element in the hot weather, but deserted now. It's a rather shallow beach and I've caught fish here just twice—the first time when a school of small stripers moved in close and I happened to be there, and the second time a couple of Octobers ago when I took a 28 pounder, one of the biggest fish I ever took from the surf, at the row of rocks that mark the northerly end of the beach.

A couple of hundred yards beyond this is Stinky Beach, so called because the shoreline takes a right angle turn, creating a corner where seaweed piles up and rots after every storm. Try along here if there's no weed in the water. Walk along the shoreline out to the rocky point that extends into the ocean. A great spot for bass, blues, and tautog.

Now, up the road another several hundred yards you'll see an old wooden gate with a narrow path behind it. Chances are there will be other cars parked there, empty rod racks on their roofs. At the end of this narrow path, ledges run down into the surf, a long rocky shoal runs out to the left, and just beyond that is a cove. Fish anywhere here. On a low tide you can work your way out to the tip of the shoal provided the surf isn't burying the rocks. When the tide is high that cove often contains bass and bluefish which are cornering bait. If you happen to be there at the right time you'll have to make a few trips back to the car to carry the fish.

For the next couple of miles north on Route 1A there are only three access roads, Newton Avenue, Hazard Avenue, and one un-named lane which you'll never find. It appears to be an entrance to one of the many large estates facing the ocean front. This is the high banks section of the coast where ledges form a solid bulwark against the relentless surf. Any place along this stretch of shoreline can be good fishing. It's probably the most heavily fished section of the Rhode Island coastline.

You can stop your car anywhere along the next half mile because the road runs right along the sea wall. Fish might come in anywhere. Just park, grab your rod, jump the wall and start fishing if you see birds working. The old Coast Guard Tower with its distinctive arch over the road is your next stop. A rocky point is your fishing platform.

Next to that is the Narragansett Town Beach, not a very good place to fish because it is a flat, shallow beach with the waves breaking far out. Drive past the first part, past the traffic light, and park in one of the fenced-in lots facing the beach. Now you've got a quarter of a mile walk to the mouth of Narrow River where predators wait for the goodies to be swept out to sea and tumbled in the rip.

You've driven less than six miles from your first stop and walked perhaps another mile, covering, in the process, just about every kind of surf condition you'll ever meet.

But that's not all of Rhode Island's surf fishing by any means. If you drive south on Route 1 you will find some great beach and jetty fishing. A series of roads lead to the water. All are well marked.

The first leads to East Matunuck Beach and the West Wall of the Point Jude Harbor of Refuge. It was off this wall that I caught my first striper, and blues, fluke, tautog and scup are caught here regularly. Fluke abound over the hard sand bottom on the outside of the long jetty.

Next is Matunuck Beach and Deep Hole where the state has provided a parking lot for surf fishermen. It's a cobblestone beach with several bars that can be waded at low tide. At Deep Hole the surf breaks against a steep, sandy beach. The first stripers of the season are generally caught here in April and fishing remains good all summer.

Farther along is Charlestown Beach, several miles of steep ocean front beach that has a road running directly in back of the dunes that border the shore. It's a dirt road with some soft spots, but your family car will make it. At the end of the road is a large state parking area and facilities for campers. This is the Charlestown Breachway, one of the most popular casting spots along the coast, partly because it is easy to reach and partly because a lot of people catch a lot of fish here. Fishermen drift live eels down the outgoing tide from the small jetty and regularly take fish of 40 pounds or more from May to November.

Trouble is, there's not much room on the jetty. When the bass are running, fishing from it becomes a body contact sport. Gets a little hairy out there on a dark night with a tight knot of fishermen casting two-foot-long eels rigged with 5/0 hooks. I prefer fishing the beach. Squid, cut herring or mackerel, eels or worms are used from the beach with good effect. The area is set aside for fishermen, by the way. You won't be bothered with swimmers and sun bathers here.

From Charlestown you can continue south and turn in at Quono-chontaug where there is another state-maintained fishing area— Green Hill, Weekapaug, Misquamicut and Watch Hill. You'll see as many Connecticut as Rhode Island cars along here. Nutmeg State anglers who have few surf fishing opportunities in their own state flock to this area.

For its size Rhode Island probably offers a greater variety and more opportunities for surf fishing than any of the coastal states. From Narragansett to Watch Hill is a drive of about 25 miles. If you were to stop and give every spot a good try, it would take you all summer.

Furthermore in most places the state sees to it that there are access points and visiting anglers will have little trouble finding places to fish.

Watch Hill is the last stop in Rhode Island. I've never fished beyond that into Connecticut for a couple of reasons. One is that much of the Connecticut shoreline fronts on Long Island Sound rather than on the open ocean and does not offer true surf fishing. Once past New London you are out of the high surf country. Furthermore, from what I have been able to observe, most of the state's shoreline is not easily accessible. Private beaches and town-owned beaches restricted to the use of residents discourage wide use by visitors.

LONG ISLAND

So we'll jump across the sound to Long Island where you'll find all the surf fishing you can handle.

If you're going in from New England, by the way, there's no need for that horrendous drive through New York City. A ferry runs from New London to Orient Point and another runs from Bridgeport to Port Jefferson. The last time I was there the fare was $20.50 for a car, the driver and one passenger, and if you feel the same way I do about driving through New York City — it's worth it.

If you intend to take the New London-Orient Point ferry on a weekend call ahead for reservations. I failed to do this on one of my trips and spent a frustrating three hours waiting for an opening.

Except for Montauk Point's rocky tip, just about all of Long Island's southern shoreline is barrier beach, some of it easily accessible to surf fishermen, some accessible only to those with beach vehicles. Some is open to all, some spots are seasonally restricted to residents, and some areas are state parks where surf fishing is permitted under certain regulations. There is approximately 120 miles of beach between Brooklyn and Montauk. An angler can stand almost anywhere and cast with a reasonable expectation of catching something or other. A volume would be required to catalog all the available surf fishing opportunities.

If you intend to do much surf fishing on Long Island I suggest subscribing to a weekly publication called *The Long Island Fisherman*. It carries weekly reports of fishing activities in all areas as well as articles on when, where, and how to fish by some knowledgeable fishermen. Its one weakness as far as I'm concerned is that it relies heavily on the reports of charter and head boat skippers whose success, or lack of success, does not always relate to what's happening along the beach. Its reports from Montauk, for instance, invariably tell what's happening with the extensive charter fleet there. Rarely does it give surf fishing reports for Montauk.

It does carry advertisements of many bait and tackle shops in every area, however, and the people who run these places can be tapped for information. In the past dozen years I have visited many of Long Island's beaches; fishing mostly those that can be reached without the aid of four wheel drive. These are the ones I'll report on:

We'll start with Montauk Point, a rock-knuckled fist that jabs the North Atlantic and piles up the breakers. Montauk is famous for its charter fleet which carries thousands of fishermen daily to these waters to reap what seems to be an inexhaustable supply of gamefish. The boats don't get them all. There's plenty left for us.

A couple of large parking lots at Montauk Lighthouse (free parking before and after the summer tourist season) and some well-trodden paths give the surf fisherman convenient access to the shoreline. Here we encounter our last rocky beaches on our trip down the coast.

The light itself sits on a high bluff. Directly below the light and on either side fishermen will find some rough but fishable water.

There's a lot of shoreline here that can be reached on foot. A good place to start is to the left of the light where there's a cove and then a bar. You can work your way all the way out to False Point about a half mile to the northwest, fishing as you go. There is a road that runs along the shore here, but it is barely passable for a standard car. Four wheel drive is recommended. If you start to the right of the light you can fish around the point for about a half mile to a place called Turtle Cove. That's as far as you can go because of the Air Force Base. There's no road along here; it's all hiking.

You can get the hottest, up-to-date fishing information easily enough. Just park your car in the lot close to the cars of other fishermen and get acquainted. Most of them, like fishermen everywhere, are friendly and will be happy to help a visiting fisherman. A couple of times I established friendships here that led to invitations to go along in a beach buggy, thus opening opportunities to fish country I'd have missed. Another good source of information is Johnny's Bait and Tackle, the hangout for local surf fishermen. It's on the right just after you pass the center of Montauk Village.

Montauk is easy to reach. Just follow Route 27 until you can't go any farther without pontoons and you're there. The Montauk area offers other surf fishing opportunities, but I have not sampled all of them.

But I have sampled some. Moving back from the point along the Montauk Highway you'll pass Fort Hero; then you'll come to the community of Ocean Side. Turn in there. There's a town beach you can fish in spring and fall. This is the Ditch Plains area; sand beaches liberally sprinkled with boulders.

Back at Montauk Village you might find good fishing anywhere along the beach. It was here that I woke up in my beach-front motel one September morning and saw birds wheeling over the water. I landed and released a dozen or more small bluefish and three or four squeteague before breakfast.

Between Montauk Village and Hither Hills State Park a few miles to the east you can travel the Old Montauk Highway. Access to the beach is limited along here because you have to cross private property, but there are a few places where you can park and walk in. If you have a four-wheel drive you can roam the beach at will.

If you have a camper, there's a big campground at the state park. You can find good fishing right at the campground. You're not welcome at the bathing beach during the summer, but you're free to fish there after the bathers have gone for the season.

About eight miles west of Hither Hills I found an isolated stretch of Napeague Beach uncluttered by cottages or any other sign of life except beach fishermen and an occasional pair of young lovers. I found it by wondering one day as I drove past what was at the end of some sand roads that seemed to lead off toward the dunes. I parked beside the road and walked in. It's about a quarter of a mile over the dunes to the beach, a long way to haul a 30 pound striper or a string of big bluefish to be sure. Don't try to drive the family car in over these roads. You won't make it.

There are miles of beach here and you can fish as much of it as your legs will allow. On the several occasions I've hiked in, only a few beach buggies were cruising and looking for fish. Except for that day on my fall trip last year. The beach buggies were clustered at a spot close to where I crossed the dunes. They were into a school of weakfish that had moved in with the late afternoon tide and were chasing bait close to shore. For more than an hour we had fishing about as fast as I've ever experienced. I could have had more except that one of the buggies going off the beach just about dark offered me a ride back to my car. Crossing the dunes and finding the car in the dark could have been a problem.

With so many miles of beach to fish, a Long Island fisherman is like a kid in a candy store. The visiting fisherman is in a worse position than the native, since all he sees is miles of beach on a map with no way of knowing which tiny spot on the map represents a good place to cast a line.

I use two methods. Besides the Original Boyd Fishfinder Method involving finding a place where a bunch of others are fishing, the second method is just as simple. Fish the inlets. If the fish are going to be anywhere, it's at the inlets.

On a barrier beach such as Long Island's south shore there are inlets which permit the passage of water, and fish, between the ocean and the rich bay waters. An inlet is, in effect, a bottleneck. The fish may be spread out in the ocean or in the bay, but when they pass through the inlet they've got to be close to where you can catch them. The narrow water forces them to bunch up. Furthermore, as mentioned before, the rich aquatic life of the inland waters is spewed out in a great, natural chum line when the tide runs out, setting the table for predator fish.

Let's concentrate on Long Island's inlets. The first and easiest to reach is Shinnecock Inlet, the southern entrance to the Shinnecock Canal allowing boat passage from the ocean through Great Peconic Bay to Long Island Sound. It also permits passage of fluke, stripers, blues, weaks, kingfish, winter flounder, tautog and a great lathering of lesser creatures.

A plugger works the surf at Shinnecock, Long Island, where waves break close to shore

There are two ways to get to Shinnecock Inlet. From the east turn off Route 27 at Southampton and follow the beach road to the inlet. During the summer parking here is restricted to residents of Suffolk County, but in spring and fall the restriction is lifted. From the west turn off at Hampton Bays and then turn left when you hit the beach road. Here there are no parking restrictions.

The jetties on either side provide casting platforms if you want to fish the swirling waters of the inlet. Or the beaches on either side can be productive.

Getting to Moriches Inlet, the next one down, can be something of a problem but well worth it. From Shinnecock Inlet you simply drive west along the beach road to the end of the road. That's as close as you can get without four wheel drive. There's a parking lot at the end of the road where you can leave your car. Then it's a mile and a half hike.

I found the inlet to be rather shallow with enough rocks to make bottom fishing hazardous and a swiftly-flowing tide. Nevertheless a companion and I caught fluke on strip baits during the daylight hours, tied on bucktail jigs when the sun dipped low, and caught blues and weaks. When it got dark we went to swimming plugs. Our only reward was a small striper that Jerry almost landed. The fish flipped off as he was beaching it and landed in the water before either of us could grab it.

A day later I struck up a conversation with some buggy drivers who were going onto the beach at Smith Point Park and heading for the west side of the inlet. Nobody offered me a ride so I hiked down the beach a ways, baited with sea worms, and caught absolutely nothing.

The westerly side of Moriches Inlet is something over seven miles from Smith Point Park, a large and popular park under the jurisdiction of Suffolk County. You need a permit to get on the beach here. They are obtainable at the park.

Fire Island Inlet is a little closer to a parking lot.

The Robert Moses State Park is the closest you can get to Democrat Point which is the seaward side of the Fire Island Inlet. You get to the state park by turning off Route 27 at Brightwaters. Once in the park, go to the right to Parking Area 2. Leave your car there, walk past the pitch and putt golf course, and Democrat Point is something less than a mile away. A permit obtainable at the park office is needed if you intend to fish after dark.

Sometime in the near future an extension of the road and a new parking lot are planned which will enable you to drive closer to the point which is the western most end of Fire Island. There's now beach buggy passage to the point. You must stop at the park office and have the buggy inspected before you go out.

You don't need to go out to the point to get big fish, though. The beach to the west of the bathing beach is a favorite spot for fishing live eels either night or day, although night is considered the best time.

The other side of Fire Island Inlet can be fished from a protuberance called The Sore Thumb at Oak Beach. It's just a short distance from the causeway that brought you out to Robert Moses State Park. However Oak Beach is seasonally restricted to town residents and there is a fee charged. Off season it's free. The last time I was at the Sore Thumb was mid-September of last year. Anglers were scoring on weaks using cut bait on the bottom. Three or four years ago I found kingfish there.

There's another inlet at Jones Beach 15 miles to the west, another at Atlantic Beach and still another at Rockaway Beach. I have never fished any of them, having a strong aversion to fishing so close to large population centers. It is for this reason that I have never fished some pretty good beaches on Boston's North Shore and have skipped over the Atlantic City area when fishing New Jersey.

I know, I'm missing some good fishing by skipping these places, but there is so much available in less crowded areas where I'm quite a bit happier. One time I did decide to try fishing some of the places I'd read about close to the New York Metropolitan area. It didn't work out. A September afternoon at Sandy Hook, New Jersey, the fishing was only fair. I still had two days left before I had to get back to the office. I decided to see some of these beaches for myself.

After leaving Sandy Hook about 4 p.m., I drove north to the New Jersey Turnpike, crossed Staten Island, and took the Verrazanno Bridge to Brooklyn, where I made a wrong turn and got hopelessly lost.

I'm a small town boy, used to towns that have one main street. Places like Brooklyn purely frighten me. After it was almost dark, I found myself in a section called Bensonhurst, a bewildering grimy place whose sidewalks were jammed with people who had never walked on anything but concrete. A service station attendent at last directed me to the Shore Parkway, my original goal. Here I wasn't much better off. The parkway was jammed with cars driven by suicidal drivers. Once among them I had no chance to slow down to read signs or turn off to stop and consult a map. Finally, in desperation, I made a right turn which miraculously turned out to be what I was looking for, a road that would take me to the beach areas. Now I could find a motel, put up for the night, and explore the fishing the next day.

Two hours later, after driving confused, tired, hungry, and with a growing headache through a misty rain, I was somewhere out on Long Island. I had passed through the Rockaways, Atlantic Beach, and Long Beach without finding a motel. So I headed inland again, hoping to find a place to eat and sleep on one of the main east-west roads. It was some time after 9 p.m. before I found a motel in Massapequa Park that was located, I found out, near the railroad station. Did you know the trains on the Long Island Railroad run all night? They also blow their horns whenever they approach a station.

It was still raining the next morning so I drove to Port Jefferson and caught the ferry to Bridgeport and got home a day early. That's why I've never fished the western end of Long Island.

NEW JERSEY

I could direct the reader to good surf fishing in New Jersey by simply saying start at Sandy Hook, drive south, turn into any of the thousand or so streets that dead end at the beach and start fishing.

That's the kind of a place New Jersey is. It's mostly barrier beach, all 120 miles of it, with a number of openings into the shallow, fertile bays behind the beach. There aren't many places where you can't fish, and no matter where you are, the fishing is usually good.

Most of the beaches are controlled by the towns which means that rules and regulations change every few miles. In some places parking near the beach is either prohibited or non-existent, particularly during the summer season. Most places relax their rules after Labor Day.

All but a few miles of the waterfront are lined with cottages, motels, boardwalks, amusement parks and other evidences of a large population which places a premium on being near the ocean. Only at Island Beach State Park has the state moved in to preserve the shoreline and the dunes.

More than 60 years ago Van Campen Heilner, one of the outstanding outdoor writers of his day, wrote of Barnegat Light, *"Situated on a desolate spit of sand, surrounded by vast salt marshes, the light and its few little houses, called by the ironical name of Barnegat City, is typical of Southern New Jersey and its inhabitants—Exposed to sunshine or storm it leads a solitary existence, but a hardy one."* (From *Call of the Surf* by Van Campen Heilner and Frank Stick, published 1920 by Doubleday, Page & Co.).

Not any more. Today Barnegat Light is a state park with a large parking lot that is crowded daily during the summer months. Motels, pizza palaces, hot dog stands, and other establishments do a rushing business where there was only "a desolate spit of land" half a century ago.

Heilner writes of pitching his tent on the deserted beach at Harvey Cedars just down the road from Barnegat. There are no more deserted beaches at Harvey Cedars either. Cottages stand shoulder to shoulder along the beach front.

No, New Jersey has little in the way of isolated shoreline today; but even its crowded, cluttered, sometimes honky-tonk beachside communities have some of the best surf and jetty fishing anywhere. The state has, moreover, some of the hardest-fishing surf men I've ever come across.

There's only one section of the New Jersey coast I haven't fished. That's the area around Atlantic City, Margate City, and Ocean City, not because there isn't good fishing there, but simply because, as mentioned earlier, I can't hack those crowded areas. I understand there is good fishing right at Atlantic City's famed Boardwalk and that Brigantine, just to the north, may be one of the best surf fishing spots in the state.

There is a weekly publication similar to *The Long Island Fishermen* published in New Jersey. It's called, as you might expect, *The New Jersey Fisherman*. It employs the same format as its counterpart except that one section is devoted to shore fishing reports. If you intend to do much fishing in New Jersey, buy it.

Both magazines carry weekly tide tables, by the way.

A trip down the coast would begin at Sandy Hook, a park of the Gateway National Recreation Area. It's located just beyond Atlantic Highlands on Route 36, the coastal highway.

The National Park Service has set aside several fishing areas. Admission to the park is free. Fishermen take fluke, weaks, bass and sometimes kingfish all summer long. In the fall, stripers, blues, and weaks storm the beach as they chase schools of bait. Spring and summer baits are worms, squid and cut bait. In the fall, cut or whole

The rip just to the south of Barnegat Light

mullet are popular. Plugs, tin, and bucktail jigs score heavily on feeding fish. It's a steep beach with the surf breaking directly on the shore and deep water, by surf fishing standards, close in.

Just to the south are Sea Bright and Monmouth Beach, a couple of seaside communities sitting precariously behind high sea walls. Old timers tell of the times the sea broke through to inundate the narrow neck of land between the ocean and the Navesink and Shrewsbury Rivers. You can fish from these sea walls if you can find a place to park. The ocean breaks at the base of the wall in some places, in other places the sand has been moved in to form narrow beaches. Jetties provide casting platforms along the shore as well.

From Monmouth Beach south to Brielle and Point Pleasant there is a sameness to the shore. Jetties, many holding a fisherman or two, interrupt the beach at regular intervals through Long Branch, Deal, Asbury Park, Bradley, Belmar, Spring Lake, and Sea Girt.

In some places you park your car close to a jetty, but parking is not permitted on all streets leading to the ocean front. This will be your first problem in fishing this area, finding a place to leave your car. In Long Branch and Asbury Park there are boardwalks lined with parking meters. Parking restrictions are relaxed in some towns after the summer season, but better inquire locally before you walk away from your car. In some places the no parking restriction is enforced the year around.

These North Jersey jetties and beaches yield up catches of fluke and weaks all season, with enough stripers and blues around to keep it interesting. Blues and weaks linger until well into October and some stripers insist on staying until November and even into December. The New Jersey striper season officially closes on December 31. Some are still being taken right up until then. I met one fisherman who boasted he has baked stuffed striped bass for Christmas dinner every year. Tautog are present along the jetties until early November.

The coast is interrupted between Bradley Beach and Belmar by Shark River Inlet, a place that has treated me well. The north jetty has a spur that runs parallel to the beach, a fishing platform that gives access to some productive water. It was from the spur in September of 1973 that I caught an eight and a quarter pound fluke, the largest one I've ever caught. On an October night a couple of years earlier, under a bright harvest moon, I caught and released stripers until it wasn't any fun any more.

Manasquan Inlet at Point Pleasant is another spot that shouldn't be missed. A large parking lot will accommodate your car. A walk across the broad beach will bring you to the end of the inlet's south jetty.

A mixed bag of fluke and weaks on a Jersey jetty.

The inlet here is churned by the propellors of countless boats, both pleasure and commercial craft. It is the northern entrance to the Inland Waterway and Brielle, to the north of the inlet, docks more commercial fishing vessels and charter boats than any other port on the coast.

You can fish the north jetty, too. I've seen fishermen out there, but I've always fished the beach at the south jetty.

I should emphasize here that all my trips to Jersey were in the spring or summer. These North Jersey beaches, all close to large urban areas, are too crowded for me between Memorial Day and Labor Day. Furthermore many towns put on restrictions against surf fishing during the bathing season.

South of Manasquan the character of the beach front changes somewhat. Now it is mostly summer colony country. Route 35 runs along the ocean front through Bay Head, Mantolocking, Lavallette and Seaside Heights before reaching the single naturally-preserved section of shoreline on the whole New Jersey coast. Private homes block access to the beach through most of Mantolocking and Lavallette, but at Seaside Heights you can pull up your car on any of the dead end beach streets and fish.

Surf fishing is permitted here, but it's carefully regulated. You can't fish the park between Memorial Day and Labor Day. There's a botanical preserve and a bathing beach there, but that section is open to fishermen the rest of the year. You must get an annual fishing permit to fish anywhere in the park. The permit enables you to fish around the clock. If you don't have one, you've got to get out by 8 p.m. Or, if you have a beach buggy, you can get a permit that allows you to run the entire beach.

There is an entrance fee of $1.00 for each vehicle plus 25¢ for each person. To get into the lower end of the park it will cost you another quarter for each person between Memorial Day and Labor Day. If you have a beach buggy you can get a $20 season pass that takes care of all fees for the year.

There are parking areas and dune crossing points all along the lower road, so you don't really need a beach buggy unless you intend to fish down to the north jetty of Barnegat inlet and even then it isn't entirely necessary. You can walk in from the end of the road, something less than a mile.

The north jetty has been described as the best place to fish on the entire New Jersey Coast, which may just be that. Stripers, blues, weaks, fluke and tautog come often and in large sizes off the north jetty including many bass over 30 pounds, a blue last year that went over 20 pounds, doormat-size fluke and those big ol' white chinner tautog.

The north jetty fishing improved a couple of years ago when the Army Corps of Engineers built up a large section to provide a fishing platform that reaches well out into fish-filled water. Prior to that the jetty was partly submerged. Now fishermen (the smart ones wearing creepers on their soles) can walk the flat-topped rocks for a considerable distance and, for that matter, may have to because of the popularity of the jetty.

Any of the fishing methods used elsewhere along the coast are profitably employed here, with eels a favorite of those who seek big bass. When the hordes of migrating bass and blues begin to hit this coast in the fall, many turn to plugs and jigs.

The jetty was improved because of a shoaling situation in the inlet. Whether this situation is improved I don't know, but it did change the fishing on the south side of the inlet near Barnegat Light. The fishing there is no longer as productive as it once was. The change in the north jetty and the resulting alteration of the inlet's currents have left the south jetty high and dry. A few years ago I caught stripers in deep water off the south jetty. Today the south jetty stands clear of the water altogether and the channel is farther from shore.

The south side of the inlet is still immensely popular with weekend fishermen. Fluke, weaks, snapper blues and an occasional striper fall to the bait fishermen who line the shore. Before Memorial Day and after Labor Day there is no charge for parking in the large state parking lot and many of the cars parked there will have empty rod racks on their roofs. Some rock ledge and a jetty just in back of the light are favorite spots. The beach along in front of the jetty that once fronted on the water has its quota of fishermen.

But the best beach fishing is no longer at the inlet. Try just a little to the south. What you do is drive back to Eighth Street in Barnegat City, go in and park at the end of the road. It's just a short walk over the dunes to the beach. Just to your right is the rotting remains of an old pier and bulkhead. Fishermen cast plugs or soak bait on either side of this. Another 200 yards south the mast of a sunken boat sticks up out of the surf. Just beyond that is a rip formed by a sand bar. You'll find fishermen here any evening or early morning. Most cast cut bait or worms, but some ply the white water with plugs, tin or bucktail jigs.

The north jetty of Barnegat inlet is only a few long casts away from the south jetty, a couple of minutes flight by a sea gull. But by road it's more than 30 miles. You've got to go back to Seaside Heights and take Route 37 out to the Garden State Parkway, drive south to Route 72 where you'll turn east to Long Beach Island. Barnegat Light and the south side of the inlet are ten miles north.

Long Beach Island stretches south for 20 miles from Barnegat Light, offering surf fishing at almost any point along the way. I counted almost 300 access roads to the water one rainy day a few years ago, and you can park at the ocean end of almost any of them.

All the beaches are closed to beach buggies from May 30 to September 30 and, depending on what township you're in, there is an annual fee for running the beach. The only township which does not permit beach buggies is Barnegat Light, but with plenty of access to the water you won't need one anyway.

The last mile on the southern tip of the island is Holgate, a barren section preserved as a bird sanctuary, but open to surf fishermen either on foot or aboard a four-wheel drive vehicle. You can park your car at a parking lot at the end of the road and fish all the way to the inlet. The southern tip of the island looks out over Beach Haven Inlet which opens into Little Egg Harbor.

Van Campen Heilner and Frank Stick caught channel bass here 50 years ago, but I could find no one who had caught or seen one among modern day fishermen.

There are jetties at regular intervals all along the island, but they are not the high jetties found in other parts of the state. While they are not high enough to provide fishing platforms, they are enough to create eddies and rips that attract fish. The rule all along the island is to fish the north side of any jetty. I can offer no explanation for this, nor can I testify that the north side is any better than the south side. I've caught fish on both sides.

As I mentioned earlier, on all my trips to Jersey I've missed the crowded Atlantic City, Margate City, Ocean City area. My usual course when traveling south is to leave Long Beach Island, get on the Garden State Parkway, and stay on it to exit 25 which brings me back to the shoreline just south of Ocean City.

Now I've got 25 miles of shoreline to fish between there and Cape May; some of it excellent, some of it not so good. Too much of this area is now solidly lined with summer cottages, motels, amusement parks, and other clutter, so much so that large sections of the beach are now cut off. One rather short stretch of beach is still open and free from intrusion. At Whale Beach in Sea Isle City you can park almost any-where along the road, climb over the low dune, and fish the wide, shallow beach.

Whale Beach is the kind of a place where you bait up, cast and wonder what will hit next. In early fall mixed catches might include stripers, blues, weaks, fluke, and kingfish. You'll almost always find someone fishing there to give you some tips on what fish are hitting and what they're hitting on.

The only other place along that stretch of shoreline I've fished is at North Wildwood where the beach makes a right angle turn to head into Hereford Inlet. I've stopped off here several times because every time I've been there, either spring or fall, people are fishing and

A fisherman unhooks a small blue at Whale Beach, South Jersey, to add to the fluke and weaks already caught.

catching something. There are jetties and beaches and a popular sea wall where fishermen line the rail daily. Fluke and weaks are the prime targets in the spring, in the fall small bluefish are added to the stringers, along with occasional stripers. Kingfish were once taken here, but in recent years I haven't seen any.

Cape May, the southernmost community in New Jersey, is the first place to catch migrating fish in the spring and the last to lose them in the fall. It's mostly jetty fishing here. Almost any jetty along the waterfront is likely to hold fishermen, but the most popular one by far is the southernmost rockpile on the waterfront.

Weakfish and fluke are taken in the spring, along with a few stripers. A few blues summer here, along with the weaks and fluke, and then in the fall the blues move in. Southward migrating stripers join them and jetty fisherman haul mixed strings off the jetties until cold weather closes in.

The south jetty at Cape May gets crowded when the fish are biting.

Cape May, like Montauk to the north and Ocean City, Maryland to the south, is heavily oriented toward boat fishing. Charter and head boats fish both the Atlantic Ocean and Delaware Bay sides of the cape for weaks, blues, and fluke. In April the boats put out for the offshore migration of mackerel and into Delaware Bay for the spring run of black drum. A shore fisherman will also occasionally hook a black drum, but hardly anybody fishes for them from the shore.

DELAWARE

Across Delaware Bay is the tiny state of Delaware which, more than any state along the coast, has taken care to preserve its shoreline. The state has only about 24 miles of coastline on the Atlantic from Cape Henlopen to Fenwick Island and almost half that is under state control. Rehoboth Beach is the only sizeable community on the coast. The towns of Bethany Beach, South Bethany, and Fenwick also interrupt the shoreline.

Cape Henlopen State Park pokes its finger into Delaware Bay and offers several miles of surf fishing on the ocean side. It's just west of the town of Lewes where the Cape May Ferry docks. Turn left when you get off the ferry and you're there. Ask at park headquarters about the surf fishing.

Route 14 hits the Delaware Coast just south of Rehoboth Beach and carries you south to the Maryland line. There's surf fishing off Rehoboth Beach and Dewey Beach and if you stop off at Herb's Bait and Tackle on Route 14 in Dewey Beach he'll tell you where to go and what to use for bait.

When you leave Dewey Beach you enter the Delaware Seashore State Park. In the park, access to the beach is limited to designated dunes crossings at state parking lots, but there are enough of them so that you can fish most of the beach by hopping from place to place. Before Memorial Day and after Labor Day there is no charge for parking.

Beach buggies are permitted, but you need a permit. There are wheel-marked dunes crossings for vehicles. With a buggy you can hit anyplace on the Delaware shore.

Indian River Inlet, which connects the sea with a large inland bay system is one of the most popular fishing spots on the Middle Atlantic Coast. The state maintains a large campground nearby and there is a large parking lot for day visitors as well as bath houses and concessions.

In spite of the fine fishing, I avoid the place during the summer and on weekends in spring and fall. It's just too blamed crowded. The Old Inlet Bait and Tackle Shop a mile or so north of the inlet will provide you with bait and information.

There is no sure thing in fishing, of course, but about the closest to it is to fish the end of the south jetty at Indian River Inlet on a late September morning at high tide. Use a bucktail jig with a strip of porkrind, squid, or fish belly. Last year they had great success streaming an ordinary plastic worm on the hook of a bucktail jig. Weaks, fluke, and blues were taken. For stripers, try drifting sand bugs along the jetty after dark. Use just enough weight to sink them below the surface. If it's tautog you want, put on some weight and sink the sand bug to the bottom.

And if it's dangerous living you want, fish the end of the south jetty on a Sunday morning during the vacation season.

The state park runs south for about a mile from Indian River. A point about half way down is a hot spot, but since there is no dunes crossing there, it is not heavily fished. It's a bit of a hike either from the inlet or from the first dunes crossing below.

Between Bethany Beach and Fenwick is another three mile stretch of state beach, but there are fewer access points here and crossing the dunes is forbidden. There are several dunes crossings for beach buggies.

No Parking signs limit beach access in the towns of Fenwick and Bethany Beach, but if you can find a place to park your car, you can fish anywhere. You don't have to worry about "private" beaches in Delaware.

I haven't tried to single out many particular spots along the Delaware shore because the entire shoreline is uniformly good. Enter the beach at any of the designated dunes crossings, and you should find good fishing right in front of you. Or if you want to be alone, walk a few minutes in either direction.

As mentioned earlier, most surf fishermen in this area use bait rather than artificial lures. The current along these beaches isn't strong—so all you'll need is some bottom rigs with two or three ounce pyramid sinkers. Bait with cut mullet or worms and use a float to keep the bait off the bottom. Weaks, bass or blues, and sometimes fluke can be taken here with this simple rig. Artificial lures come into their own when the big fall migration of bass and blues arrives.

MARYLAND

Maryland presents some wide contrasts in surf fishing. You can fish along the waterfront of Ocean City, one of the most popular and heavily-developed stretches of shore on the coast, or you can move south a few miles and fish lonely and wild Assateague Island.

I've tried both. Let's start with Assateague.

To get to Assateague drive west out of Ocean City on Route 50. Turn left on Route 611 and follow it over the bridge and causeway onto the island.

The Assateague Island State Park begins right there. The state maintains a stretch of the island about ten miles long. Below that it's the National Seashore.

If it's summertime, better check at the park office before slipping into your waders. Some of the beach here is set aside for bathers during the summer season. But there is plenty of beach left for surf fishing. Walking over the dunes is permitted at marked crossings only, and the rangers are strict in enforcing this rule. Once on the beach you can roam at will as long as you don't intrude on the bathing areas.

On my first visit to the park in May a few years ago, a park ranger directed me to a hole just to the left of the northernmost dunes crossing. This spot, he said, had been producing for early season anglers. It produced a couple of fluke and some weakfish for me. A visit there the following October found a school of blues frolicking along that section of beach.

To fish the National Seashore, follow the road maintained by the federal government to the sign that tells you only four wheel drive vehicles may pass. Park there, go over the dunes to the beach, and start fishing. The amount of beach you cover is limited only by the amount of walking you're willing to do. Carry some bloodworms and maybe some squid or mullet in with you.

If you have a beach buggy there's 15 more miles of National Seashore below to the Virginia State Line, all of it fishable.

One reason Assateague is of interest to many fishermen is because it is the northern limit for channel bass. Many reference books give New Jersey as the northern limit for these great surf fish, but I've found no justification for this in recent years. Van Campen Heilner wrote of catching many channel bass at Barnegat and Brigantine, but in all my travels along the Jersey coast I've never met anyone who had ever caught one.

I've seen only one, a fish of about 20 pounds being taken off Assateague by a couple of fishermen in a beach buggy. They would say only that they caught it, "down the beach aways," which was hardly pin pointing the spot.

The Ocean City Chamber of Commerce tells me that some channel bass are taken from the surf right at the city's water front every spring. I've yet to meet anyone who has caught one there, but who am I to suggest that Chambers of Commerce are sometimes over-optimistic when they get talking about the old home town.

While on Assateague, by the way, keep your eye out for the wild ponies. They're among the island's most popular residents.

Back in Ocean City you have your choice of fishing the beach or the inlet. The inlet is often the best bet, although when the fish are running well it can get crowded. There's a parking lot alongside the jetty and you can drop your line just a short distance from your car.

Ocean City in the summer, I suspect, is an horrendous place. Even in the spring and fall it hosts many vacationers. Of late it has become a popular convention city.

The beach at Ocean City extends from the inlet all the way to the Delaware State Line. From the inlet to 40th Street there's a boardwalk. Beyond that the shore front is an almost continuous line of high-rise apartments, condominiums and motels. Much of the architecture is modernistic and garish. The whole waterfront gives the impression of a high-rise slum in the making. As beauty is in the eye of the beholder, so must ugliness be. My personal viewpoint is, if you will permit a little editorializing here, that if, when The Creator made barrier beaches, He was asked what is the worst thing man could do to one, He'd have said, "Build an Ocean City." Still, the beach is there, and you can fish it wherever you can get to it.

It's a straight beach, no jetties, with not much to distinguish one part from another. Furthermore holes, sloughs, and bars move around with winter storms so that the bottom changes from year to year in any given spot.

But there are fish in the surf at Ocean City. I caught my first kingfish here a few years ago at 15th Street, right in front of the motel where I was staying (off season rates because it was after September 15). It was late morning and I had just returned from beating the surf at Assateague. I was tired and hungry. My immediate plans called for a shower, lunch, and then a nap, but when I looked out the window there was a man hauling something from the surf. Being of a nature that puts a chance to catch a fish before showers, lunches, naps, etc., I went back to the car, got waders and rod, and went out to the beach. The man, I learned, had just caught a kingfish. I had a few worms left over from the morning's fishing so I baited up, cast, and the rig had no sooner hit bottom than a pound and a half king tried to make off with it.

Most of Ocean City's fishing fame comes from its offshore sport fishery which had its birth in the 1930's when the sea broke through what is now Ocean City Inlet. This separates Assateague from the mainland and provides a convenient access to the sea for the boats docked in the area's inland waters. Fishermen putting out from Ocean City soon discovered fantastic offshore fishing for bonito, white marlin (Ocean City claims the title of White Marlin Capital of the World), dolphin, albacore, and tuna. The port and its reputation mushroomed. Today a large charter fleet puts through the inlet daily.

Interestingly, when I was there in September of 1975 as a part of the city's bicentennial celebration, all the port's charter and head boats paraded along the beach front one evening. It was an impressive sight.

Bait and tackle shops in the area, I found, are stocked with gear for the boat fishermen. In addition to the offshore fishery, a large fleet of small boats fishes the inland waters for fluke, weaks, school bass and small blues that find the inner bays an easier way of life than the open ocean.

While there are miles of open beach available, it seems most visitors and natives too, for that matter, seem to prefer boat fishing. This is all right with me. Leaves more room on the beach for us.

So there it is, about 500 miles of coastline covered in a single section. Of necessity it is sketchy, fragmentary, but it provides a starting point for someone looking for a place to fish the North Atlantic surf. I do not apologize for its failure to be more specific. Anyone using the above guide can reach whatever section of coast is most convenient for him. After that it's up to the individual to nose around, get the current dope on what's happening—the tides, the bait most likely to succeed at that time, etcetera. Bait and tackle shops are often good sources of information. I've named a few that were particularly helpful, but I've found some that were not very reliable. Some are overly optimistic in their reports in hopes of selling some bait or perhaps a lure or two. The profit motive is still very much alive in America. Local fishermen, I've found, are more helpful. Once they find you are a visiting fisherman, they are surprisingly candid in giving information. Most have pride in their local fishing and want to see visitors catch fish.

Not all, of course. Tom Morrison recalls when he first started surf fishing he ran into just such a one. Tom and his two brothers had driven to Orleans on Cape Cod to fish Nauset Beach. Directly in front of the parking lot was a lone fisherman with his rod propped in a sand spike.

"Nothing doing here," the fisherman said, "All the fish are up at the inlet. Too far for me to walk, though. Got a bad leg. But if I was you young fellows I'd hike up there. It's only a fifteen minute walk." (It's something more in the order of a 45 minute walk, by the way, but Tom had no way of knowing that).

The three started out when Jack, Tom's older brother, discovered he'd left something in the car and decided to walk back to get it. The others waited. When Jack returned he was breathless from walking and cursing.

Back at the parking lot he had found the lone fisherman disinterring six fine stripers he had buried in the sand. The three brothers had been standing on the temporary graves while the fisherman was telling them, "Nothing doing here."

He was atypical. Yet, local rivalries are apt to stop the lips of fishermen when it comes to disclosing to other local fishing rivals where and how a catch was made. In fact secrecy and downright deception are practiced unashamedly.

On my first visit to Montauk Point a dozen years ago I spread a map of the area on the hood of my car and asked a local fisherman if he could direct me to some good fishing. He was helpful, gave me details on how to get to several places he recommended and then pointed to a spot and said, "See right there, that little point. Best spot around for stripers. Not many know about it so keep it a secret, will you? We don't want too many fishermen out there."

If I had been a local fisherman I suspect he would not have confided in me.

No, I'm not telling where that point is. That's our secret.

All I have done in this book is tell you how to get to some of the places I have fished and a little of what to expect when you get there. Part of the joy of fishing is seeking out new places, discovering new methods, and making them work. At least it has been true for me.

If you live anywhere in the northeastern United States you are within driving range of the places I've described. Pick your spot, follow the directions, and you'll get there. The rest is up to you.

Section 7

To Fish the Surf...

When the president of the White Water Striped Bass Club asked if there was anything to be brought up under new business it was just a matter of form. He didn't really expect anyone to have any new business. The purpose of the WWSBC was not business, but as a gathering place for surf fishermen between fishing trips, a clearing house for information and a forum for lies. The real business of the WWSBC was surf fishing and the members knew how to attend to that on their own. They didn't need Roberts Rules of Order.

But on this night one of the younger members stood up and said, yeah, he had something to bring up, and without any preliminaries to prepare the membership for the shock said, "I move we change the bylaws to permit fresh water fishermen in the White Water Striped Bass Club."

There was a brief, stunned, unbelieving silence.

Fresh water fishermen in the WWSBC? Fresh water was for bathing and mixing with bourbon, not for fishing. Everyone was stunned.

Open a vein in any member of the WWSBC and you'd get brine.

Slit him and beach sand would spill out.

The silence ended; then it was a while before the president could gavel the meeting to order. The membership of the WWSBC was an unruly bunch anyway, and with a cockamamie proposal like this on the floor everybody had something to say and everybody wanted to say it at the same time. Except for old Burt who was as deaf as a wharf piling, and he added to the din by shouting, "What did he say? What did he say?"

When things finally quieted down, Ernie Clark, our parlimentarian, ruled the motion out of order on the grounds of damfoolishness because who wanted a bunch of la-de-da fly fishermen cluttering up the place with their buggy whip rods and mosquito wing lures, but the president overruled him. He said the motion was in order, if ill-advised, and that if anyone had the guts to second it he would put it up for discussion. Somebody had the guts and the debate was underway.

155

To summarize: The pros, who were clearly in the minority, held that good sportsmanship required that the club accept fresh water fishermen who, after all, form an important, if misguided, segment of the great fishing fraternity. Once they became members, the argument went, these men could be introduced to surf fishing, whereupon they would certainly mend their ways, give their willow wands to their wives and daughters, arm themselves with proper, man-sized gear, and go fishing for fish that had not been hand fed from birth and trained to eat anything a human being might throw to them. Furthermore, the argument went, there are among fresh water fishermen people who are responsible citizens who could be depended upon to pay their club dues on time. If there was anything the WWSBC needed any more than a new refrigerator for the beer, it was members who paid their dues on time.

But the cons, who were not only in the majority but counted among their number most of the old timers who were used to communicating above the roar of the surf, had some persuasive, and louder arguments as well. Archie Morgan summed it up this way: "I ain't takin' no lady-fingered twerp of a fresh water fisherman out on the beach with me to wet nurse. If any of them pollywog fishermen want to learn to fish the surf let 'em learn some other place. This ain't no seminary, by God. It's a surf fishin' club for surf fishermen and we already got too many people in it who spend too much time bottom grubbin' for sand dabs and cod and other such junk fish and I don't have to name no names, either. They all know who they are. Anyway, we don't need no more fishermen on the beach. Too crowded already!"

And old Burt, who was finally made to understand, stomped off muttering something about joining the Ladies Aid Society at the church. The motion lost 19 to 7 on a show of hands.

The old timers brought home a point. You learn surf fishing by surf fishing. All this book can do is serve as a starting point. What my 35 years of surf fishing have taught me can be useful to you. Yet in the final analysis, it's your own experiences, your own observations, your own trial and error that will make you a success.

What are the qualifications? Well, let's see—

You need an immunity to discomfort that permits you to keep fishing when there is sea water in your waders, sand in your molars, dryness in your throat, acute tendonitis in your right shoulder, a blister on your right forefinger if you're spinning or a groove in your left thumb if you're using a revolving spool reel, fire in your reddened eyes, and a constant ache where the spine enters the skull.

You need a mulish obstinacy that will keep you going long after the tide has turned, the appointed hour of your return home has past, and anyone with any sense at all has already quit.

You must have a casual attitude toward home, job, and other worldly responsibilities that permits you to keep on fishing without thought of any.

You should acquire a passion for lonely beaches, sunrises over the ocean, the smell of air that has traveled a thousand miles touching nothing but wave tops, the taste of salt spume on your lips, the tumult of waves crashing the shore, the tug of the backwash against your legs, the feel of a gamefish bucking at the end of a long line, the challenge of meeting and conquering your prey in its own element.

You should have an attitude of complete indifference to the attitudes of a society that looks upon surf fishermen as a fraternity of misfits because, Pal, if you're a surf fisherman, that's just what you are — a social misfit. But don't let it worry you.

Given these and a few other qualities, a person has a chance of making it as a surf fisherman. Then all he's got to do is learn the trade, so to speak.

Tell you what. You go out and get yourself a surf fishing outfit, read this book again, take whatever advice you feel is appropriate, go out and log some beach time, and I'll put you up for membership in the White Water Striped Bass Club.

Then, my friend, you'll be a surf fisherman!

Other STONE WALL PRESS Outdoor Books:

BACKPACKING FOR TROUT
by Bill Cairns
228 pages, fully illustrated, $16.95 clothbound

"This must certainly be the most complete guide to trout fishing and backpacking available. Both the novice and experienced sportsman are sure to find a great deal of useful material."

Massachusetts Audubon Society

A wealth of practical information for successful fishing away from crowded, less productive trout waters — by the founder of the famous Orvis Fly Casting School.

*   *   *   *   *

THE NATURAL WORLD COOKBOOK:
Complete Gourmet Meals from Wild Edibles
by Joe Freitus
320 pages, fully illustrated, $25.00 clothbound

At long last we have a complete and comprehensive cookbook of wild, edible foods for the adventuresome gourmet. This is the result of more than fifteen painstaking years of collecting recipes and experimenting with wild foods. Both plants (Alpine Bilberry to Wintercress) and animals (fish, fowl, and game) are included, along with beautiful line drawings for their easy identification by Salli Haberman. You will find hundreds of recipes for complete meals that can be prepared from abundant wild foods found across North America.

*   *   *   *   *

GOOSE HUNTING
by Charles Cadieux
208 pages, fully illustrated, $16.95 clothbound

A life long waterfowl hunter and outdoor writer artfully interweaves lively, personal stories of goose hunting from Quebec to Mexico with an encyclopedia of facts about good management, good goose hunting and goose watching. With humor and warmth Cadieux covers the controversy about short-stopping, goose calling and its champions, all kinds of decoys, the migration paths of geese, banding, types of geese, and much more.

*   *   *   *   *

BACKWOODS ETHICS:
Environmental Concerns for Hikers and Campers
by Guy and Laura Waterman
178 pages, $7.95 paperback

" . . . undeniably important. They argue that hikers and backpackers must protect natural resources and maintain the 'spirit of wildness' of our country's backwoods . . . they describe a new code of backwoods ethics they feel is necessary to accommodate the increasing number of hikers in the wilds."

Publishers' Weekly

Ask for these books at your bookstore or tackle dealer, or send your check for the total list amount plus $2.00 (shipping and handling) to:

STONE WALL PRESS, INC.
1241 30th Street, N.W., Washington, D.C. 20007